chef WAN

simply sedap 2

Chef Wan shares more favourite recipes

chef WAN

simply sedap 2

Chef Wan shares more favourite recipes

Chef Wan *8/8/2015*

mc Marshall Cavendish Cuisine

The publisher would like to thank Kitchen Culture Sdn Bhd for the use of their premises for the photos on cover and page 6; Barang Barang Pte Ltd, Lim's Art and Living, Royal Selangor and Sia Huat Pte Ltd for the loan and use of their tableware.

Food photography: Jambu Studio
Cover image and page 6: Pacino Wong of You Studio

Published by Marshall Cavendish Cuisine
An imprint of Marshall Cavendish International

Other Marshall Cavendish Offices:
Marshall Cavendish Corporation. 99 White Plains Road, Tarrytown NY 10591-9001, USA · Marshall Cavendish International (Thailand) Co Ltd. 253 Asoke, 12th Flr, Sukhumvit 21 Road, Klongtoey Nua, Wattana, Bangkok 10110, Thailand · Marshall Cavendish (Malaysia) Sdn Bhd, Times Subang, Lot 46, Subang Hi-Tech Industrial Park, Batu Tiga, 40000 Shah Alam, Selangor Darul Ehsan, Malaysia

Marshall Cavendish is a trademark of Times Publishing Limited

National Library Board Singapore Cataloguing in Publication Data

Wan, Chef, 1958-
Simply sedap 2 / Chef Wan. – Singapore : Marshall Cavendish Cuisine, 2012, c2006.
p. cm.
Includes index.
ISBN : 978-981-4361-53-8

1. Cooking. I. Title.

TX714
641.5 -- dc22   OCN761361410

Printed in Singapore by Fabulous Printers Pte Ltd

CONTENTS

SOUPS

SOUR AND SPICY PRAWN SOUP

Note

The fish stock in this recipe can be home-made (see pg 13), ready-made, or made by dissolving fish stock cubes or granules in water according to the manufacturer's directions for the quantity needed. If making the stock at home, you can add the heads and shells from the prawns (shrimps) in this recipe as well.

INGREDIENTS

Coriander (cilantro)	1 bunch
Bird's eye chillies (*cili padi*)	3
Fish stock (see note)	250 ml (8 fl oz / 1 cup)
Galangal (*lengkuas*)	4 thin slices, peeled
Lemon grass (*serai*)	1 stalk, finely sliced
Kaffir lime leaf (*daun limau purut*)	1, torn or bruised
Button mushrooms	2, small, quartered
Prawns (shrimps)	3, shelled, with tails intact, and deveined
Fish sauce	1½ Tbsp
Sugar	¼ tsp
Thai roasted chilli paste (*nam prik phao*)	¼ tsp
Lemon juice	1 Tbsp

METHOD

- Wash and drain coriander well, then cut off leafy tops and reserve for garnishing. Coarsely chop remaining stems and roots.

- Finely pound chopped coriander stems and roots with chillies using a mortar and pestle.

- Bring stock to the boil in a saucepan. Add galangal, lemon grass, lime leaf and pounded ingredients. Return to the boil.

- Add all remaining ingredients, except lemon juice and coriander leaves, and boil for 1 minute.

- Stir in lemon juice and switch off heat. Garnish as desired with coriander leaves and serve hot.

BOUILLABAISSE
FRENCH SEAFOOD SOUP

INGREDIENTS

Firm white fish (any kind)	1, whole, about 700 g (1½ lb)
Clams	300 g (10 oz)
Leek	1 stalk
Orange	½
Olive oil	90 ml (3 fl oz / 6 Tbsp)
Onion	1, large, peeled and finely chopped
Garlic	3 cloves, peeled and smashed
Ready-packed bouquet garni	1 sachet, or wrap 1 sprig thyme, 1 sprig parsley, 2 bay leaves and 2 leek leaves, as reserved, in clean cloth and tie with string to secure
Fennel	½ bulb, thinly sliced
Dry white wine (optional)	125 ml (4 fl oz / ½ cup)
Saffron threads	a pinch, soaked in enough hot water to cover
Salt	to taste
Freshly ground black pepper	to taste

METHOD

- Prepare seafood. Fillet whole fish, reserving head, central bone, tail and fins. Cut fillets into chunks and refrigerate until needed. Scrub clams clean, rinse well and drain; set aside.

- Prepare fish stock. Put reserved fish parts into a large pan and add 2 litres (64 fl oz / 8 cups) of water. Bring to the boil and simmer for 15 minutes, then strain and reserve. Discard fish parts.

- Trim green leaves off leek stalk and reserve 2 for home-made bouquet garni, if using. With a sharp knife, make a deep slit along the length of leek stalk and rinse off any sand trapped inside, then slice.

- Grate skin of orange with a small grater to obtain orange zest. Alternatively, peel orange carefully with a sharp knife and shred the peel. Be mindful to avoid the white portion as it is bitter.

- Heat oil in a large pan and sauté onion, garlic and leek until softened. Add orange zest, bouquet garni, fennel and wine, if using, or an equal amount of fish stock. Simmer until liquid is reduced by half.

- Add remaining fish stock and saffron, both threads and soaking liquid. Bring to the boil and simmer for 15 minutes, then add fish fillets and simmer for 3–4 minutes.

- Add clams and continue to simmer until fish flakes easily when tested with a fork. Remove seafood with a slotted spoon and transfer to a soup tureen or divide among individual serving dishes or bowls.

- Season soup to taste with salt and pepper, then ladle over seafood and serve.

OYSTER SOUP

Note

Use any type of milk, from full cream to low- or non-fat, for this recipe. It is really question of your health concerns or taste preferences. You can also use cream in place of milk for an even richer taste.

INGREDIENTS

Oysters	12
Butter	150 g (5 oz)
Onion	1, peeled and finely diced
Celery	1 stalk, finely diced
Plain (all-purpose) flour	4 Tbsp
White wine (optional)	250 ml (8 fl oz / 1 cup)
Fish stock	1 litre (32 fl oz / 4 cups), use ready-made (see pg 10) or home-made (see pg 13)
Milk	1 litre (32 fl oz / 4 cups)
Thyme	3 sprigs
Paprika (optional)	2 tsp
Salt	to taste
Ground white pepper	1 tsp or to taste

GARNISHING

Chives	1 small bunch

METHOD

- Shuck oysters, if still in their shells, then rinse and drain well. If preferred, chop oysters into small pieces for a stronger oyster-flavoured soup.
- Heat butter in a pan and fry onion and celery until softened, then add flour and stir for 2 minutes.
- Add white wine, if using, or an equal amount of fish stock and deglaze the pan: use a wooden spoon to loosen all the brown bits stuck to the pan and stir constantly until they are dissolved and liquid becomes uniform in colour.
- Add remaining stock, milk, thyme and paprika, if using. Season to taste with salt and pepper and simmer for 10 minutes.
- Remove thyme and discard, then add oysters and simmer for about 3 minutes or until they are cooked. Be careful not to overcook oysters as they become tough and dry.
- Garnish as desired with chives and serve. Traditionally, this soup is served with a sprinkling of chopped chives.

VICHYSSOISE
POTATO AND LEEK SOUP

Note

Whenever chicken stock is mentioned in this book, it can be home-made; ready-made in Tetra Paks or cans; or made by dissolving stock cubes, granules or concentrate in water according to the manufacturer's directions for the quantity needed. To make your own, boil chicken necks, backbones and/or wing tips in water. For a more western-style stock, add some chopped vegetables, such as onion, carrot, celery and leeks, and strain before using or storing.

INGREDIENTS

Butter	4 Tbsp
Onion	1, large, peeled and diced
Leeks	6 stalks, use white portions only, cleaned and sliced (see pg 13)
Potatoes	4 large, peeled and diced
Chicken stock (see note)	2.5 litres (4 pints / 10 cups)
Bay leaf	1, or 2 dried bay leaves
Double (heavy) cream	1 small carton, about 145 ml (5 fl oz)
Salt	to taste
Ground white pepper	to taste

METHOD

• Melt butter in a pot. Add onion and leeks and sauté until softened but not brown.

• Add potatoes, stock and bay leaf. Simmer until potatoes are soft.

• Remove and discard bay leaf, then transfer soup to a blender (processor) to purée.

• Pour puréed soup into a clean pot and bring to a simmer. Stir in cream, then season to taste with salt and pepper.

• Remove from heat and serve warm or at room temperature, if preferred. This soup, however, originated as a summer dish and was served chilled.

WINTER MELON SOUP

Note

Vegetable pear, true to its name, looks like a large pear but flattened. It has green skin and whitish flesh, and is used much like squash in cooking. The fruit vegetable is also known by the names of choco and fut sau kwa, *Cantonese for "Buddha's hands gourd".*

INGREDIENTS

Cooking oil	1 Tbsp
Garlic	1 clove, minced
Ginger	2-cm (1-in) knob, peeled and shredded
Shiitake mushrooms	450 g (1 lb), stems removed and halved or quartered
Oyster mushrooms	150 g (5 oz), sliced
Shelled prawns (shrimps)	150 g (5 oz), deveined
Winter melon flesh	200 g (7 oz), cut into cubes
Vegetable pear (chayote)	½, peeled, cut into cubes
Water	2.5 litres (4 pints / 10 cups)
Chopped spring onions (scallions)	a handful
Coriander leaves (cilantro)	a handful
Salt	to taste
Ground white pepper	to taste
Egg	1, beaten

METHOD

- Heat oil in a wok or large saucepan. Fry garlic, ginger and both types of mushrooms until fragrant.
- Add prawns, winter melon and vegetable pear. Cook for 5 minutes over low heat.
- Add water, spring onions and coriander. Season to taste with salt and pepper. Simmer for 10 minutes or until melon pieces are tender.
- Swirl egg into soup just before serving.

PUMPKIN SOUP

Note

If you plan on garnishing the soup as suggested and the brand of salted fish you are using happens to be very salty, rinse it or soak it in some water to remove excess salt. Be mindful to drain salted fish well, if soaking, and dry with paper towels before frying. This is because moisture in the salted fish will cause the hot oil to sputter, which not only makes a mess of your stove top, but may give you painful blisters as well.

INGREDIENTS

Green apples	2
Butter	4 Tbsp
Onion	1, peeled and finely diced
Pumpkin	½, medium, peeled, seeded and diced
Tom yum paste	3 Tbsp
Canned tuna	1 can, about 170 g (6 oz), drained
Coconut cream (see pg 31)	250 ml (8 fl oz / 1 cup), preferably squeezed from 1 grated coconut
Chicken stock (see pg 16)	2.5 litres (4 pints / 10 cups)
Ginger	2-cm (1-in) knob, peeled and bruised
Lemon grass (*serai*)	1 stalk, bruised
Chopped coriander leaves (cilantro)	a handful, chopped
Salt	to taste
Sugar	to taste

GARNISHING (OPTIONAL)

Salted fish	50 g (2 oz), finely diced and crisp-fried
Coconut cream (see pg 31)	4 Tbsp
Ready-made chilli oil	to taste
Finely diced green apple	as reserved

METHOD

- Core green apples and peel, if desired. Finely dice flesh and reserve some for garnishing, if using.
- Heat butter in a pot and fry onion and pumpkin until softened.
- Add all remaining ingredients, except coriander leaves, salt and sugar. Simmer for 15 minutes.
- Remove ginger and lemon grass and discard. Stir in coriander leaves, then transfer to a blender (processor) to purée.
- Pour puréed soup into a clean pot and bring to a simmer. Season to taste with salt and sugar just before serving.
- Ladle into individual serving bowls. Garnish, if using, as desired with crisp-fried salted fish, coconut cream, chilli oil and reserved green apple.

SALADS & VEGETABLES

LADIES' FINGERS AND MINT SALAD

Note

As far as possible, use young and tender ladies' fingers for this recipe. If using more mature ones, cut off and discard their stem-tops, which can be tough and fibrous. To dry-roast dried prawn (shrimp) paste, place it in a dry pan over low heat and use the spatula to break it up into smaller pieces, then stir them around until deeply aromatic. Dried prawn paste can be dry-roasted in larger quantities and stored in an airtight container for future use.

INGREDIENTS

Ladies' fingers (okra)	30, blanched and thickly sliced
Onion	1, medium, peeled and chopped
Prawns (shrimps)	200 g (7 oz), boiled until cooked and shelled, with tails intact
Mint leaves	a handful
Torch ginger bud (*bunga kantan*)	½ stalk, finely sliced
Fish sauce	4 Tbsp
Kalamansi limes (*limau kesturi*)	4, squeezed for juice
Grated palm sugar (*gula Melaka*)	2 Tbsp or to taste

SPICE PASTE

Red chillies	5, seeded, if desired, and thickly sliced
Dried prawns (shrimps) (*hae be*)	4 Tbsp, rinsed clean, soaked in water to soften and drained
Garlic	2 cloves, peeled
Tomatoes	2, quartered
Dried prawn (shrimp) paste (*belacan*)	2 tsp, dry-roasted (see note)

METHOD

- Combine all spice paste ingredients in a blender (processor) until smooth.
- Place ladies' fingers, onion, prawns, mint and torch ginger bud in a mixing bowl. Toss with spice paste until evenly mixed.
- Add fish sauce, lime juice and palm sugar. Toss to mix well and adjust seasoning to taste, if necessary. Serve immediately.

SQUID AND MANGO SALAD

INGREDIENTS

Squid tubes	300 g (10 oz), cleaned
Fish sauce	2 tsp
Garlic	2 cloves, peeled and chopped
Ground white pepper	to taste
Olive oil	2 Tbsp

GARNISHING

Dried prawns (shrimps) (*hae be*)	225 g (7½ oz / 1½ cups), rinsed clean, soaked in water to soften and drained
Cooking oil	125 ml (4 fl oz / ½ cup)

SALAD INGREDIENTS

Unripe mangoes	2, peeled and cut into thin strips
Ripe mango	1, peeled, seeded and cut into thin strips
Shallots	10, peeled and thinly sliced
Bird's eye chillies (*cili padi*)	5, sliced
Tomatoes	3, seeded and sliced into strips
Kaffir lime leaves (*daun limau purut*)	2, central stems removed and shredded
Lemon grass (*serai*)	1 stalk, thinly sliced
Mint leaves	a handful

DRESSING (COMBINED)

Fish sauce	125 ml (4 fl oz / ½ cup)
Grated palm sugar (*gula Melaka*)	6 Tbsp or to taste
Limes (*limau nipis*)	2, squeezed for juice

METHOD

- Prepare squids. Carefully slice open a squid tube so it can lay flat and cut a lattice pattern on the softer, internal surface. Repeat with other squid tubes.

- Season squid pieces with fish sauce, garlic and pepper to taste, then leave to marinate for 20 minutes.

- Meanwhile, prepare garnishing. Dry pre-soaked dried prawns with paper towels and heat oil in a small saucepan. Fry prawns until golden brown and crisp. Remove and drain on paper towels.

- Heat olive oil in a pan over high heat and sear marinated squid for 30 seconds; it should turn white and curl. Remove and slice into desired serving size pieces.

- Put all salad ingredients in a large bowl. Add squid pieces and toss with dressing until evenly mixed, then divide into individual serving portions.

- Garnish as desired with dried prawns and serve immediately.

CHICKEN AND COCONUT SALAD

Note

Kerisik *is made by dry-frying grated skinned coconut over low heat for 30–40 minutes until it turns dark brown and fragrant, not burnt. It is then finely pounded. Because it takes much time and effort to prepare, many cooks have the habit of making extra to store in airtight containers. Crisp-fried shallots are thinly sliced shallots that have been fried in hot oil until golden brown. Both* kerisik *and crisp-fried shallots can be bought ready-made.*

INGREDIENTS

Chicken breast meat	280 g (9½ oz)
Salt	to taste
Ground white pepper	to taste
Cooking oil	2 Tbsp + enough for deep-frying
Firm bean curd (*tau kwa*)	2 pieces
Fermented soy bean cake (*tempe*)	4 pieces

SPICE PASTE

Red chillies	8, seeded, if desired, and thickly sliced
Bird's eye chillies (*cili padi*)	4, seeded, if desired
Shallots	8, peeled
Garlic	3 cloves, peeled
Lemon grass (*serai*)	2 stalks, sliced
Kaffir lime leaves (*daun limau purut*)	2, central stems removed and sliced
Candlenuts (*buah keras*)	6

DRESSING

Vegetable oil	4 Tbsp
Coconut cream (see pg 31)	250 ml (8 fl oz / 1 cup), preferably squeezed from 1 grated coconut
Grated palm sugar (*gula Melaka*)	4 Tbsp
Fish sauce	3 Tbsp
Limes (*limau nipis*)	2, squeezed for juice

SALAD INGREDIENTS

Cucumber	½, peeled, if desired, and sliced into circles
Pineapple	¼, peeled and sliced crossways into triangular shapes
Long (snake) beans	10, blanched and diagonally sliced
Crisp-fried shallots (see note)	1 Tbsp or to taste
Grated skinned coconut	150 g (5 oz / 2 cups), for making *kerisik* (see note)
Turmeric leaves (*daun kunyit*)	2, shredded

METHOD

- Lightly season chicken with salt and pepper. Heat 2 Tbsp oil in a pan and fry chicken for 2–3 minutes on each side or until cooked and lightly browned. Remove and allow to cool.

- Heat sufficient oil for deep-frying. Add firm bean curd and fry until golden brown, then remove and drain on paper towels.

- Lower fermented soy bean cakes into the same oil and fry until golden brown. Remove and drain on paper towels.

- Slice cooked chicken into desired serving size pieces; set aside. Cut fried bean curd into square quarters; set aside. Slice fried fermented soy bean cake crossways into 1-cm (½-in) strips; set aside.

- Combine all spice paste ingredients in a blender (processor) until smooth.

- Prepare dressing. Heat oil in a wok or large saucepan over medium-low heat and fry blended spice paste until fragrant. Add coconut cream and bring to the boil, then simmer until sauce thickens. Add palm sugar, fish sauce and lime juice. Stir through, switch off heat and allow to cool completely.

- Meanwhile, prepare salad ingredients and put all of them in a large bowl.

- Add chicken and deep-fried ingredients and toss with desired amount of cooled dressing until evenly mixed. Transfer to a serving dish or bowl, garnish as desired and serve immediately.

CHICKEN AND COUSCOUS SALAD

Note

Although many cooks use pre-cooked or instant couscous, some feel that the richer taste and texture of unprocessed couscous deserve the extra time and effort. Instant couscous is the most commonly used option and it should be cooked according to packet instructions, which may vary slightly from brand to brand. Generally, however, it involves adding couscous into hot water and allowing to stand until all the water has been absorbed and the grains puffed up.

INGREDIENTS

Chicken breast meat	350 g (11½ oz), excess fat trimmed and cut into bite-size pieces
Cooking oil	1 Tbsp
Mixed salad leaves	300 g (10 oz)
Cherry tomatoes	8, halved, if desired
Walnuts	150 g (5 oz), or 165 g (5½ oz) almonds
Pears (any kind)	2, peeled, if desired, cored and cut into wedges
Cooked couscous	320 g (10½ oz / 2 cups)
Basil leaves	a handful

DRESSING

Balsamic vinegar	4 Tbsp
Dijon mustard	1 tsp
Sugar	1 tsp
Garlic	2 cloves, peeled and minced
Extra virgin olive oil	125 ml (4 fl oz / ½ cup)
Red chilli	1, seeded and minced
Lemon grass (*serai*)	1 stalk, minced
Torch ginger bud (*bunga kantan*)	1, finely sliced

METHOD

- Pan-fry chicken in oil until lightly browned, then remove and set aside.
- Prepare dressing. Put all ingredients into a bowl and stir until well-blended and sugar is dissolved.
- Put all other ingredients, including fried chicken, in a large bowl. Add desired amount of dressing and toss until evenly mixed.
- Transfer to a serving dish or bowl and serve immediately.

ASPARAGUS SALAD

Note

Fresh coconut cream can be bought from the refrigerated section of certain supermarkets. Coconut cream in cans and Tetra Paks are more readily available than its fresh counterpart. Alternatively, squeeze about 75 g (2½ oz) grated skinned coconut for about 60 ml (2 fl oz / ¼ cup / 4 Tbsp) fresh coconut cream. One skinned coconut is about 300 g (10 oz) when grated, and gives about 250 ml (8 fl oz / 1 cup) coconut cream when squeezed.

INGREDIENTS

Asparagus	300 g (10 oz), lower ends trimmed and peeled, if outer layer is fibrous
Prawns (shrimps)	15, boiled until cooked and shelled, with tails intact
Grated skinned coconut	150 g (5 oz)
Onion	1, peeled and sliced
Coconut cream (see note)	3 Tbsp
Pointed pepper leaves (*daun kaduk*)	a handful, sliced

DRESSING

Red chillies	4, seeded, if desired, and thickly sliced
Dried prawn (shrimp) paste (*belacan*)	1 tsp, dry-roasted (see pg 22)
Sugar	2 tsp or to taste
Salt	½ tsp or to taste
Kalamansi limes (*limau kesturi*)	5, squeezed for juice
Kaffir lime (*limau purut*)	½, grated for zest

METHOD

- Prepare dressing. Either finely pound or blend (process) chillies and dried prawn paste together. Stir sugar and salt into lime juice until dissolved, then mix with blended chillies and lime zest.
- Put all other ingredients in a mixing bowl and toss with dressing until evenly mixed.
- Transfer to a serving dish or bowl and serve immediately.

PUMPKIN AND PRAWN SALAD

Note

To obtain tamarind juice, stir tamarind pulp in hot water and strain; a more concentrated juice gives a tarter taste and vice versa. If unsure, always make a little more than is called for in a recipe, and make it more concentrated rather than less. This is because it is easier to dilute its flavour in a dish with some water or counter it with some sugar, than to make more juice while cooking. After a few tries, you will know the proportion that suits your taste.

INGREDIENTS

Peeled pumpkin	200 g (7 oz), cut into desired serving size pieces
Olive oil	to taste
Cracked black pepper	to taste
Mixed salad leaves	150 g (5 oz)
Coriander leaves (cilantro)	1 bunch
Prawns (shrimps)	5, shelled, with tails intact, and deveined, then steamed or boiled until cooked
Bird's eye chillies (*cili padi*)	5 or to taste, sliced
White sesame seeds	2 tsp, dry-roasted (see pg 35)

DRESSING

Grated palm sugar (*gula Melaka*)	½ Tbsp
Lime (*limau nipis*) juice	1 Tbsp
Fish sauce	1½ Tbsp
Tamarind (*asam Jawa*) juice (see note)	1 tsp or to taste
Garlic	1 clove, peeled and finely chopped
Lemon grass (*serai*)	3 stalks, thinly sliced
Kaffir lime leaf (*daun limau purut*)	1, central stem removed and shredded
Shallots	2, peeled and finely sliced
Mint leaves	6, chopped + 1 small sprig for garnishing
Chopped coriander (cilantro) leaves	1 Tbsp

METHOD

- Put pumpkin in a roasting pan and season with olive oil and pepper. Oven-roast pumpkin at 180°C (350°F) for 20 minutes or until slightly softened.
- Prepare dressing. Stir together palm sugar, lime juice, fish sauce and tamarind juice in a bowl, then mix in remaining ingredients.
- Line a serving dish or bowl, which can be a hollowed out pumpkin, with salad and coriander leaves, then top with prawns and spoon dressing over.
- Garnish as desired with chillies, sesame seeds and mint. Serve immediately.

TROPICAL CHICKEN SALAD

Note

Dry-roasting certain ingredients, such as cashew nuts, sesame seeds and whole spices, enhances their aroma and flavour. To dry-roast an ingredient, place it in a dry pan over low heat and stir constantly until it is slightly darker in colour and fragrant. Some books refer to dry-roasting as toasting. Also, instead of dry-roasting small quantities as they are needed, you could dry-roast a larger quantity and store in an airtight containers for future use.

INGREDIENTS

Chicken breast meat	300 g (10 oz), excess fat trimmed and sliced into bite-size pieces
Cooking oil	1 Tbsp
Cucumber	1, cored and cut into bite-size pieces
Pineapple	1, peeled and cut into bite-size pieces
Spring onions (scallions)	4, thinly sliced
Tomatoes	3, cut into small wedges
Papaya	¼, peeled, seeded and cut into bite-size pieces
Onion	1, medium, peeled and thinly sliced
Cashew nuts	140 g (4½ oz / 1 cup), dry-roasted (see note)
Finely chopped coriander leaves (cilantro)	2 Tbsp
Finely chopped mint leaves	2 Tbsp

DRESSING

Limes (*limau nipis*)	2
Red chillies	2, seeded and minced
White sesame seeds	40 g (1¼ oz / ¼ cup), dry-roasted (see note)
Sesame oil	½ tsp
Fish sauce	2 Tbsp
Palm sugar (*gula Melaka*)	2 Tbsp, grated or melted in a little water
Extra virgin olive oil	4 Tbsp

METHOD

- Pan-fry chicken in oil until lightly browned, then remove and set aside.
- Prepare dressing. Use a small grater to grate zest from 1 lime into a bowl, then squeeze juice from both limes over. Add all remaining ingredients and stir until well-mixed.
- Put all other ingredients, including fried chicken, in a mixing bowl. Toss with desired amount of dressing until evenly mixed.
- Transfer to a serving bowl and serve immediately.

PECEL KEREDOK
SALAD WITH PEANUT SAUCE

Note

This recipe was inspired by Sri Owen, one of my favourite Indonesian cookbook authors and a very dear friend. She wrote Indonesian Regional Food and Cookery, *which was published in 1994 and has since won the André Simon Award. Historically, this dish originated from western Java and was popularised by the Sundanese people.*

INGREDIENTS

Long (snake) beans or French beans	10, thinly sliced
Cabbage	¼ head, small, thinly sliced
Bean sprouts	100 g (3½ oz), tailed, if desired
Cucumber	1, peeled, if desired, cored and thinly sliced
Yam bean (*bangkuang*)	1, peeled and thinly sliced
Fermented soy bean cake (*tempe*)	1, sliced and fried until golden brown
Bird's eye chilli (*cili padi*) (optional)	1, seeded, if desired, and minced

DRESSING

Garlic	3 cloves, peeled and minced
Dried prawn (shrimp) paste (*belacan*)	1 tsp, dry-roasted (see pg 22)
Lesser galangal (*cekur* or *kencur*)	2 pieces, peeled
Bird's eye chillies (*cili padi*)	10, finely pounded
Grated palm sugar (*gula Melaka*)	3–4 Tbsp or to taste
Skinned peanuts (groundnuts)	150 g (5 oz / 1 cup), dry-roasted (see pg 35) and finely pounded
Tamarind (*asam Jawa*) juice (see pg 32)	125 ml (4 fl oz / ½ cup)
Salt	to taste
Sugar	to taste

METHOD

- Prepare dressing. Finely pound garlic, dried prawn paste, lesser galangal and chillies together, then mix in all remaining ingredients. Add just enough water to reach desired consistency.

- Place long or French beans and cabbage, reserving a little of each for garnishing, in a large bowl. Add all remaining ingredients, except chilli, then toss with desired amount of dressing until evenly mixed.

- Transfer to a serving dish or bowl and garnish as desired with reserved cabbage and long beans, and minced chilli. Serve immediately.

KULAT SISIR MASAK LEMAK BERPAKU
BLACK FUNGUS AND VEGETABLE FERN IN COCONUT GRAVY

INGREDIENTS

Fresh black (wood ear) fungus (*kulat sisir*)	120 g (4 oz / 2 cups)
Vegetable ferns (*pucuk paku*)	1 bunch
Bird's eye chillies (*cili padi*)	3–4 or to taste
Turmeric (*kunyit*)	3-cm (1½-in) knob, peeled
Coarse salt	1 tsp or to taste
Lemon grass (*serai*)	2 stalks, bruised
Coconut cream (see pg 31)	250 ml (8 fl oz / 1 cup), preferably squeezed from 1 grated coconut

METHOD

- Wash and drain fungus well, then chop coarsely or grind coarsely using a mortar and pestle. Set aside.

- Wash and drain vegetable ferns well, then slice thinly and set aside.

- Finely grind chillies, turmeric and salt together, then transfer to a pot or large saucepan.

- Add lemon grass, coconut cream, black fungus and vegetable ferns. Stir through and bring to the boil, then simmer until ingredients are cooked.

- Serve warm with rice.

AUBERGINES IN TANGY SAUCE

INGREDIENTS

Aubergines (eggplants/brinjals)	600 g (1 lb 5 oz)
Cooking oil	85 ml (2½ fl oz / ⅓ cup)
Fish curry powder	50 g (2 oz), mixed with 100 ml (3½ fl oz) water into a paste
Tamarind pulp (*asam Jawa*)	100 g (3½ oz), mixed with 800 ml (26 fl oz / 3¼ cups) water and strained
Prawns (shrimps)	250 g (9 oz), medium, shelled, with tails intact
Red chillies	2, slit lengthways and seeded, if desired
Sugar	85 g (2½ oz) or to taste
Salt	1¼ tsp
Light soy sauce	2 Tbsp

SPICE PASTE

Dried chillies	15, rinsed clean, soaked in water for 10 minutes and drained
Shallots	15, peeled
Dried prawn (shrimp) paste (*belacan*)	2 tsp, dry-roasted (see pg 22)

METHOD

- Trim off tops and ends of aubergines, if preferred, then halve them lengthways and make a deep slit along the centre of each half. Soak cut aubergines in salted water to prevent discolouration. Drain well before use.
- Combine all spice paste ingredients in a blender (processor) until smooth.
- Heat oil and fry spice paste until fragrant, then add curry paste and stir-fry until it is fully incorporated and mixture is aromatic.
- Reduce heat and add aubergines, cut side down. Gently stir-fry for a few minutes until aubergines are evenly coated, then stir in tamarind juice. Bring to the boil and simmer for about 15 minutes.
- When aubergines are nearly tender, add prawns and chillies and season to taste with sugar, salt and soy sauce. Return to the boil, then remove from heat.
- Serve warm with rice.

NONI SHOOT SALAD

Note

Noni leaves are widely regarded as healthful, but they are not always easy to find. This dish makes the best of the leaf's wholesome qualities by encouraging the consumption of the leaves themselves, rather than just their juice, which is commercially available in bottles and quite costly. Although noni leaves are relatively inexpensive, their taste is rather intense and can be an acquired taste.

INGREDIENTS

Chubb mackerels (*ikan kembung*)	6, cleaned and boiled or steamed until cooked
Kerisik (see pg 26)	4 Tbsp
Young noni leaves (*pucuk mengkudu*)	8, central stems removed, thinly sliced and parboiled to soften
Shallots	6, peeled and thinly sliced
Red chillies (optional)	2, seeded, if desired, and thinly sliced
Coconut milk (see pg 60)	90 ml (3 fl oz / 6 Tbsp)
Limes (*limau nipis*)	2, squeezed for juice
Salt	to taste
Ground white pepper	to taste

GARNISHING

Bird's eye chilli (*cili padi*)	1, seeded, if desired, and finely chopped
Coconut cream (see pg 31)	2 Tbsp or to taste
Noni leaf (optional)	1, cleaned and left whole
Noni fruit (optional)	1, cleaned and left whole

METHOD

- Remove skins of cooked mackerels and discard. Separate meat from bones and place in a mixing bowl; discard bones.
- Flake fish into small chunks, if necessary, then add *kerisik* and mix well.
- Add noni leaves; shallots, reserving some for garnishing; chillies, if using; coconut milk and lime juice. Toss until evenly mixed, then season to taste with salt and pepper.
- Transfer to a serving plate and garnish as desired with reserved shallots, bird's eye chilli, coconut cream, noni leaf and noni fruit. Serve immediately.

CASHEW FRUIT SALAD

Note

Polygonum leaves are also known as Vietnamese mint, or daun kesum to Malay-speakers. They are intense in aroma and flavour—mainly warm and woody, with some bite. Because of their strength, these leaves are typically used sparingly. Probably the most famous use of polygonum leaves is in laksa, *a dish of thick rice noodles bathed in a rich gravy of spices and coconut cream. Here, a sprinkling of polygonum leaves works wonders in countering the otherwise cloying gravy.*

INGREDIENTS

Chubb mackerels (*ikan kembung*)	4, large, cleaned and boiled or steamed until cooked
Shallots	4, peeled
Kerisik (see pg 26)	55 g (2 oz / ½ cup)
Polygonum (*laksa*) leaves (see note)	a bunch, finely sliced
Ground white pepper	1 Tbsp
Red chillies	2, thinly sliced, or 5 bird's eye chillies (*cili padi*) for a more fiery taste
Cashew fruits (*buah gajus*)	6, half-ripe, roughly chopped
Salt	to taste
Palm sugar (*gula Melaka*)	4-cm (2-in) chunk or to taste, grated
Fresh coconut cream (see pg 31)	4 Tbsp
Limes (*limau nipis*)	2, squeezed for juice

METHOD

• Remove skins of cooked mackerels and discard. Separate meat from bones and set aside; discard bones.

• Pound shallots and *kerisik* until smooth using a mortar and pestle. Add mackerel and pound again until well-blended. Transfer to a mixing bowl.

• Mix in polygonum leaves, pepper, chillies and cashew fruits. Season to taste with salt and palm sugar.

• Add coconut cream and lime juice. Toss until evenly mixed, then transfer to a serving dish or bowl and serve immediately.

MOROCCAN CARROTS

INGREDIENTS

Butter	6 Tbsp
Golden raisins	80 g (2¾ oz / ½ cup)
Carrots	5, peeled, if desired, and cut into chunks
Oranges	2, squeezed for juice
Brown sugar	3 Tbsp
Salt	to taste
Ground white pepper	to taste
Mint leaves	a handful, chopped

SPICES

Ground cinnamon (*kayu manis serbuk*)	1 tsp or to taste
Ground cumin (*jintan putih serbuk*)	½ tsp or to taste
Cayenne pepper	½ tsp, or 1 finely chopped red chilli

METHOD

- Melt butter in a pot and fry raisins for 1 minute. Add carrots and season to taste with spices.
- Add orange juice and sufficient water to cover carrots. Cook over high heat until most of the liquid has evaporated.
- Reduce heat and sprinkle in brown sugar. Cook until caramelised; carrots should look glossy. Season to taste with salt and pepper.
- Dish out and sprinkle mint leaves over before serving.

SAVOURY CORN PANCAKES

Note

Egg whites are typically beaten to three different stages: soft-, medium- and firm-peak. At soft-peak stage, the foamy egg whites form a weak mound that is prone to collapsing when the beater is lifted. At medium-peak stage, the egg whites are opaque and form a relatively stable mound, but with a rounded top rather than a peak, when the beater is lifted. At firm-peak stage, the egg whites are stiffly true to their name and hold their pointed shape clearly.

INGREDIENTS

Plain (all-purpose) flour	140 g (5 oz)
Oat bran	130 g (4½ oz)
Bicarbonate of soda (baking soda)	1 Tbsp
Salt	1 tsp
Red chilli	1, seeded, if desired, and chopped
Spring onions (scallions)	3, thinly sliced
Chopped coriander leaves (cilantro)	2 Tbsp
Canned corn kernels	1 can, about 410 g (13½ oz)
Plain yoghurt	225 g (7½ oz)
Melted butter	4 Tbsp
Egg whites	2, beaten to medium-peak stage (see note)
Cooking oil	4 Tbsp

METHOD

- Put flour, oat bran, bicarbonate of soda, salt, chilli, spring onions, coriander and corn in a large bowl and mix well.
- Add yoghurt and butter, then fold in egg whites. Cover with a clean cloth and leave to rest for 10 minutes.
- Oil a griddle or flat non-stick pan and place over medium heat. Spoon ladlefuls (each about 4 Tbsp) or smaller portions, if preferred, onto hot pan.
- Allow to cook on one side until bubbles rise to the surface, then turn over and continue to cook until golden brown on both sides.
- Remove pancake and keep warm. Repeat with remaining batter until it is used up and re-oil pan as necessary. Serve as desired.

CAPONATA

ITALIAN MIXED VEGETABLE SALAD

INGREDIENTS

Olive oil	4 Tbsp
Onion	1, large, peeled and finely chopped
Garlic	2 cloves, peeled and finely chopped
Golden raisins	80 g (2¾ oz / ½ cup), soaked in water for 30 minutes and drained
Pine nuts (optional)	1 Tbsp, dry-roasted (see pg 35)
Honey	1 tsp or to taste
Balsamic vinegar	2 Tbsp or to taste
Salt	to taste

VEGETABLES

Aubergine (eggplant/brinjal)	1, medium, ends trimmed and cut into bite-size pieces
Red capsicums (bell peppers)	2, seeded, white pith removed and cut into bite-size squares
Courgette (zucchini)	1, medium, ends trimmed and cut into bite-size pieces
Celery	2 stalks, cut into bite-size pieces

GARNISHING

Basil leaves	1 small sprig

METHOD

- Heat oil in a pan. Fry onion and garlic until lightly browned. Add all the vegetables and continue to fry until just softened.

- Add all remaining ingredients and adjust seasoning to taste. Cook over very low heat, allowing vegetables to simmer gently in their own juices, for about 15 minutes or until they are tender.

- Dish out, garnish as desired with basil and serve.

MUSHROOM QUICHE

INGREDIENTS

Plain (all-purpose) flour	500 g (1 lb 1½ oz)
Cold butter	225 g (7½ oz), cut into small cubes
Lemon juice	1 Tbsp
Ice water	
Dried beans (any kind)	
Grated Parmesan cheese	100 g (3½ oz)

FILLING

Olive oil	2 Tbsp
Butter	2 Tbsp
Onion	1, large, peeled and chopped
Dried thyme	1 tsp
Button mushrooms	10, stems removed and sliced
Shiitake mushrooms	15, stems removed and sliced
Leek	4-cm (2-in) length, use white portion only, cleaned (see pg 13) and thinly sliced
Salt	to taste
Freshly cracked black pepper	to taste

CUSTARD

Eggs	5
Cream	500 ml (16 fl oz / 2 cups)
Salt	to taste
Freshly ground black pepper	to taste

METHOD

- Put flour into a mixing bowl. Add butter and use your fingers to rub it in until mixture resembles bread crumbs.
- Mix lemon juice with a little water and sprinkle over pastry crumbs. Add ice water, a little at a time, to form a soft, but not sticky, dough. Use just enough water to bind the ingredients. Cover dough with plastic wrap (cling film) and refrigerate for 1 hour.
- Meanwhile, prepare filling. Heat oil and butter in a pan and sauté onion and thyme until onion is softened and translucent.
- Add mushrooms and leek. Cook until mushrooms are softened and reduced slightly in size. Season to taste with salt and pepper, then remove from heat and set aside.
- Roll out refrigerated dough on a lightly floured surface until it is large enough to evenly line the base and sides of a 23-cm (9-in) quiche pan.
- Carefully lift dough and place it over the quiche pan, then lightly press dough into the pan so that it takes the pan's shape completely. Trim off any excess dough.
- Cover dough-lined quiche pan with aluminium foil so no part of the dough is exposed, pressing the foil in to take the shape of the pan as well.
- Fill the pan with beans, packing them in lightly to fill the cavity completely. Bake pastry case in a preheated oven at 180°C (350°F) for 20 minutes.
- Meanwhile, prepare custard. Beat eggs and cream together until well-combined and smooth, then season with salt and pepper. Set aside.
- Take baked pastry case out of the oven and do not switch off heat. Remove beans and foil, then add filling and spread out evenly. Sprinkle in cheese and pour custard all over filling.
- Return pan to the oven and bake for 25 minutes or until custard is set and cooked. Leave to cool slightly before slicing to serve.

SEAFOOD

PORTUGUESE MIXED SEAFOOD STEW

Note

The seafood used for this stew varies slightly from region to region along the country's coast. It is usually a mixture of fish and shellfish that depends on local catches and availability. White fish, such as halibut, monk fish and hake, are favoured for this stew, but red snapper, red mullet and sole make acceptable substitutes. Sometimes, salted cod (bacalhau) is also added.

INGREDIENTS

Olive oil	4 Tbsp
Onion	1, peeled and finely diced
Garlic	3 cloves, peeled and finely chopped
Leeks	2 stalks, use white portions only, cleaned (see pg 13) and sliced
Green or red capsicum (bell pepper)	1, seeded, white pith removed and cut into small squares
Carrot	1, peeled, if desired, and cut into small cubes
Potatoes	2, medium, peeled, halved lengthways, then sliced crossways
Tomatoes	4, chopped
Fish stock	1.5 litres (48 fl oz / 6 cups), use ready-made (see pg 10) or home-made (see pg 13)
Mixed seafood	400 g (13½ oz), use any combination of fish, crab, squid, prawns (shrimps) or mussels
Lemon	½, squeezed for juice
Chopped parsley	1 Tbsp

SEASONING

Finely chopped basil	2 Tbsp, or 2 tsp dried basil
Finely chopped oregano	1 Tbsp, or 1 tsp dried oregano
Bay leaves	2, or 4 dried bay leaves
Saffron threads	2 tsp
Ground paprika	2 tsp
Cayenne pepper	¼ tsp

METHOD

- Heat olive oil in a pot or large saucepan. Add onion, garlic, leeks, capsicum, carrot, potatoes and seasoning ingredients. Fry over low heat for 5 minutes.
- Add tomatoes and stir for 5 minutes or until they are softened, then add stock and bring to a simmer.
- Add seafood and simmer for 5–7 minutes, or until seafood is cooked.
- Stir in lemon juice and transfer to individual serving bowls. Garnish as desired with parsley and serve.

PORTUGUESE FISHBALL CURRY

Note

Minced fish meat can be bought ready-made from certain wet markets, while most supermarkets sell the frozen version in blocks. To make your own, you will need skinned fillets of firm fish such as Spanish mackerel or wolf herring. Use a tablespoon to scrape the fillets so they flake and remove all fine bones at the same time. Lastly, chop flaked meat repeatedly with two cleavers; pound using a mortar and pestle; or blend (process) it until it is sticky and pasty.

INGREDIENTS

Minced fish meat (see note)	500 g (1 lb 1½ oz)
Onion	1, peeled and minced
Garlic	2 cloves, peeled and minced
Green chilli	1, seeded, if desired, and minced
Egg white	1
Cooking oil	4 Tbsp
Ginger	1-cm (½-in) knob, peeled and minced
Curry leaves	2 sprigs, leaves separated and stems discarded
Coconut milk (see pg 60)	1 litre (32 fl oz / 4 cups)
Salt	to taste
Lemon	½, squeezed for juice

DRY INGREDIENTS

Fish curry powder	3 Tbsp
Chilli powder	2 tsp
Ground turmeric (*kunyit serbuk*)	½ tsp

METHOD

- Place minced fish in a large bowl. Add half the onion and half the garlic, but all of the green chilli and egg white. Mix well, then shape mixture into balls about 2.5 cm (1 in) in diameter. Set aside.
- Heat oil in a pot. Add remaining onion and garlic, ginger and curry leaves, reserving some for garnishing. Fry over low heat until fragrant.
- Put all dry ingredients in a small bowl and mix with a little water to form a paste, then add to pot and fry over low heat for about 5 minutes.
- Add fishballs and coconut milk. Bring to a gentle simmer and cook for about 10 minutes, seasoning to taste with salt.
- Add lemon juice, stir through and dish out. Garnish as desired with reserved curry leaves and serve.

FISH BOTOK-BOTOK
SPICY STEAMED FISH PARCELS

Note

The herbs listed in this recipe were once readily available in the backyards of homes in Malaysia. In view of urban living and development, this is no longer the case today. Use as many of the herbs as you can find, with the majority still obtainable from wet markets. Omitting a few will not drastically alter the taste of the final dish.

INGREDIENTS

Spanish mackerel (*ikan tenggiri*) steaks	500 g (1 lb 1½ oz), seasoned with fine salt
Banana leaves	3–5, depending on the number of steaks, each 35 x 25 cm (14 x 10 in), wiped clean and softened by soaking briefly in hot water

SPICE PASTE

Shallots	6, peeled
Garlic	4 cloves, peeled
Ginger	1 slice, peeled
Galangal (*lengkuas*)	2.5-cm (1-in) knob, peeled and sliced
Lemon grass (*serai*)	2 stalks, sliced
Dried prawn (shrimp) paste (*belacan*)	1 Tbsp, dry-roasted (see pg 22)

HERB MIXTURE

Pointed pepper leaves (*daun kaduk*)	a handful
Polygonum (*laksa*) leaves (see pg 42)	a handful
Young tapioca leaves (*pucuk ubi*)	a handful
Mint leaves (*daun pudina*)	a handful
Young fig leaves (*pucuk ara*)	a handful
Chinese moon creeper (*daun sekentut*)	a handful
Young noni leaves (*pucuk mengkudu*)	a handful
Turmeric leaves (*daun kunyit*)	a handful
Water dropwort leaves (*daun selom*)	a handful
Indian pennywort (*daun pengaga*)	a handful

SAUCE

Cooking oil	4 Tbsp
Coconut cream (see pg 31)	250 ml (8 fl oz / 1 cup), mixed with 3 Tbsp fish curry powder
Bird's eye chillies (*cili padi*)	10 or to taste, sliced
Chilli powder	1 tsp
Kerisik (see pg 26)	1 tsp

METHOD

- Combine all spice paste ingredients in a blender (processor) until smooth and set aside.

- Prepare herb mixture. Divide each herb into 2 equal portions. Take 1 portion of every herb and shred, then mix them together and set aside. Leave remaining portions as they are.

- Prepare sauce. Heat oil in a pan and fry spice paste over medium-low heat until fragrant and lightly browned. Add all remaining ingredients and stir to mix well, then add shredded herbs and continue cooking until oil separates to form a layer on top. Remove from heat.

- On each banana leaf wrapper, make a 'bed' with whole herbs, then place a fish steak on top. Spoon a generous amount of sauce over fish and wrap up, securing with skewers or kitchen string.

- Steam parcels for about 15 minutes or until cooked, then serve as desired.

SELADA UDANG RAMPAI
SPICY PRAWN AND VEGETABLE STIR-FRY

Note
The vegetables in this dish are meant to be crisp and the carrot slices, especially, are meant to be crunchy at the end of cooking. If you prefer softer carrot slices, parboil them in water before adding to the stir-fry.

INGREDIENTS

Cooking oil	4 Tbsp
Garlic	2 cloves, peeled and pounded
Ginger	1-cm (½-in) knob, peeled and pounded
Black mustard seeds	1 tsp
Chilli powder	2 Tbsp
Ground turmeric (*kunyit serbuk*)	2 tsp
Vinegar	2 Tbsp
Salt	to taste
Sugar	to taste
Prawns (shrimps)	10, large, feelers and legs trimmed and rinsed clean

VEGETABLES

Cucumber	½, peeled, if desired, and sliced
Carrot	½, peeled, if desired, and sliced
Green chilli	1, seeded, if desired, and sliced
Red chilli	1, seeded, if desired, and sliced
Onion	1, peeled and sliced
Garlic	3 cloves, peeled and halved

METHOD

- Heat oil and fry pounded garlic and ginger over medium-low heat until fragrant, then add mustard seeds, chilli powder, turmeric and vinegar. Stir to mix well, then season to taste with salt and sugar.
- Increase heat to medium, add prawns and stir-fry briskly to mix with pan ingredients. Add all the vegetables and stir-fry until prawns are cooked.
- Dish out and serve immediately.

FRESHWATER PRAWN STEW

Note

To save time, use ready-made coconut milk in cans or Tetra Paks for this recipe and others in the book. Traditionally, coconut milk is derived by adding water to once-squeezed grated coconut and squeezing a second time. The product of the first squeezing is called coconut cream (see pg 31). Certain supermarkets sell ready-packed freshly squeezed coconut cream. If available, dilute it with an equal amount of water (1:1) for coconut milk.

INGREDIENTS

Cooking oil	6 Tbsp
Coconut milk (see note)	750 ml (24 fl oz / 3 cups), squeezed from 1 skinned grated coconut with sufficient water added
Dried chillies	10, seeded, if desired, rinsed clean, soaked in water to soften and drained
Dried sour fruit (*asam gelugur*)	1 piece
Sugar	1 tsp or to taste
Salt	to taste
Freshwater prawns (*udang galah*) or large prawns (shrimps)	10, deveined, shelled, if desired, and rinsed clean

SPICE PASTE

Lemon grass (*serai*)	2 stalks, sliced
Galangal (*lengkuas*)	3 slices, peeled
Turmeric (*kunyit*)	2 slices, peeled
Shallots	4, peeled
Dried prawn (shrimp) paste (*belacan*)	1 Tbsp, dry-roasted (see pg 22)

METHOD

- Combine all spice paste ingredients in a blender (processor) until smooth. Drizzle in a little oil to help the blades turn, if necessary; this also means that you can use less oil to fry the paste later.

- Heat oil and fry spice paste over medium-low heat until fragrant. Add coconut milk and simmer, stirring regularly, until reduced by half.

- Add dried chillies, dried sour fruit and sugar and salt to taste. Return liquid to a simmer, then add prawns, stir through and simmer for about 5 minutes or until they are cooked.

- Dish out and serve immediately.

RENDANG UDANG RIAU
CURRIED PRAWN STEW, RIAU STYLE

Note

Rendang *is a culinary term familiar to Malaysians and Indonesians. It refers to a curried dish of typically beef or chicken that has been stewed for hours until the meat is tender and the gravy very thick. With seafood, however, the cooking time has to be relatively short to avoid overcooking, so the gravy is not as thick. Riau is an Indonesian province on the island of Sumatra and is one of the country's richest provinces because of its oil and natural gas reserves.*

INGREDIENTS

Cooking oil	125 ml (4 fl oz / ½ cup)
Coconut milk (see pg 60)	1 litre (32 fl oz / 4 cups), preferably squeezed from 1 grated coconut with sufficient water added
Freshwater prawns (*udang galah*) or large prawns (shrimps)	500 g (1 lb 1½ oz), deveined and rinsed clean
Hard-boiled eggs	3, shelled
Tamarind (*asam Jawa*) juice (see pg 32)	4 Tbsp
Kaffir lime leaves (*daun limau purut*)	2, torn
Salt	to taste
Sugar	to taste

SPICE PASTE

Red chillies	10, seeded, if desired, and thickly sliced
Shallots	10, peeled
Garlic	3 cloves, peeled
Ginger	1-cm (½-in) knob, peeled
Ground cumin (*jintan putih serbuk*)	2 tsp
Ground coriander (*ketumbar serbuk*)	2 tsp
Lemon grass (*serai*)	2 stalks, sliced
Galangal (*lengkuas*)	1-cm (½-in) knob, peeled
Black peppercorns	2 tsp

METHOD

- Combine all spice paste ingredients in a blender (processor) until smooth.

- Heat oil in a deep pan or wok. Fry spice paste over medium-low heat until oil separates to form a layer on top. Add coconut milk, stir through and simmer for 10 minutes or until gravy is slightly thickened.

- Add prawns, eggs, tamarind juice and lime leaves. Season to taste with salt and sugar. Simmer for about 5–7 minutes or until prawns are cooked. Dish out and serve immediately.

CHILLI TUNA

INGREDIENTS

Cooking oil	6 Tbsp
Aubergine (eggplant/brinjal)	1, ends trimmed, halved lengthways and diagonally cut into 5-cm (2-in) pieces
Canned tuna chunks	3 cans, each about 185 g (6 oz), drained
Dried prawn (shrimp) paste (*belacan*)	2 tsp, dry-roasted (see pg 22)
Tamarind (*asam Jawa*) juice (see pg 32)	250 ml (8 fl oz / 1 cup)
Water	125 ml (4 fl oz / ½ cup)
Green chilli	1, halved lengthways and seeded, if desired
Salt	to taste
Sugar	to taste

SPICE PASTE

Garlic	5 cloves, peeled
Shallots	15, peeled
Lemon grass (*serai*)	1 stalk, sliced
Galangal (*lengkuas*)	1-cm (½-in) knob, peeled and sliced
Dried chillies	20, rinsed clean, soaked in water to soften and sliced
Dried prawns (shrimps) (*hae be*)	150 g (5 oz / 1 cup), rinsed clean, soaked in water to soften and drained

METHOD

- Combine all spice paste ingredients in a blender (processor) until smooth. Set aside.
- Heat 2 Tbsp oil in a pan and lightly brown aubergine pieces on both sides, then remove and drain on paper towels.
- Heat remaining oil and fry spice paste over medium-low heat for 5 minutes or until fragrant.
- Add tuna and dried prawn paste and stir-fry to mix well, then add tamarind juice, water and green chilli. Stir through and cook until sauce thickens.
- Mix in fried aubergine and season to taste with salt and sugar. Dish out and serve warm.

CASHEW TUNA

INGREDIENTS

Cooking oil	125 ml (4 fl oz / ½ cup) + 1 Tbsp
Peeled yam (taro)	40 g (1½ oz), cut into 7-cm (3-in) sticks
Dried chillies	10, rinsed clean, soaked in water to soften and drained well
Onion	½, peeled and cubed
Canned tuna in olive oil	1 can, about 185 g (6 oz), drained
Cashew nuts	15, dry-roasted until golden (see pg 35)
Carrot	½, small, peeled, if desired, and sliced into circles
Chicken stock (see pg 16) or water	3 Tbsp
Red chillies	2, seeded, if desired, and sliced
Spring onion (scallion)	1, cut into 2-cm (1-in) lengths
Capsicum (bell pepper)	¼, seeded and cut into bite-size pieces
Basil leaves	a handful, chopped + extra for garnishing

SEASONING

Fish sauce	1 Tbsp
Oyster sauce	2 Tbsp
Sugar	1 tsp
Sesame oil	1 tsp
Light soy sauce	1 tsp
Chinese cooking wine (*hua tiao*) (optional)	3 Tbsp

METHOD

- Heat 125 ml (4 fl oz / ½ cup) oil in a pan and fry yam sticks until cooked, then drain on paper towels and set aside. Add dried chillies to the same oil and fry until aromatic. Drain on paper towels and set aside.

- Heat 1 Tbsp oil in a clean pan and fry onion for 5 seconds before adding tuna, cashew nuts, carrot, fried yam, stock or water and seasoning ingredients. Stir-fry to mix well and adjust seasoning to taste.

- Add fried and fresh chillies, spring onion, capsicum and chopped basil. Stir-fry to mix well again. Dish out and garnish as desired with extra basil. Serve immediately.

TUNA CAKES

Note

Chervil is an herb that belongs to the parsley family. Its green, curly leaves are what cooks use for seasoning. Although most supermarkets sell both fresh and dried chervil, the flavour of dried chervil pales in comparison to its fresh counterpart. Substitute 1 tsp dried chervil for 1 Tbsp fresh chopped chervil.

INGREDIENTS

Potatoes	1 kg (2 lb 3 oz), boiled until cooked, peeled and mashed
Canned tuna	2 cans, each 185 g (6 oz), drained
Smoked salmon	100 g (3½ oz), chopped
Onions	2, peeled
Red chillies	2, chopped
Garlic	2 cloves, peeled and minced
Ready-made mayonnaise	110 g (4 oz)
Crisp-fried shallots (see pg 26)	30 g (1 oz) or to taste
Chervil leaves	1 sprig, chopped, about 2 Tbsp
Salt	to taste
Ground white pepper	to taste
Butter	3 Tbsp
Olive oil	4 Tbsp

METHOD

- Combine all ingredients, except butter and olive oil, in a large bowl. Mix well and shape mixture into small patties, about 1.5-cm (¾-in) thick.
- Heat butter and olive oil in a pan until butter is completely melted, then fry patties until golden brown on both sides.
- Remove and drain on paper towels. Serve warm.

SALTED FISH AND PINEAPPLE CURRY

Note

Halba campur *is a ready-made mixture of mainly fenugreek and black mustard seeds, as well as either or both of the following: cumin and black onion seeds. If unavailable, mix together equal parts of fenugreek and black mustard seeds, then add a small sprinkling of either cumin and black onion seeds, or both, as you prefer.*

INGREDIENTS

Cooking oil	125 ml (4 fl oz / ½ cup)
Ginger	2-cm (1-in) knob, peeled and cut into thin strips
Shallots	5, peeled and sliced
Curry leaves	1 sprig
Halba campur (see note)	2 tsp
Fish curry powder	4 Tbsp, mixed with a little coconut milk into a paste
Salted fish	500 g (1 lb 1½ oz), excess salt rinsed off and cut into desired serving size pieces
Coconut milk (see pg 60)	500 ml (16 fl oz / 2 cups)
Pineapple	½, peeled and cut into desired serving size slices
Dried sour fruit (*asam gelugur*)	5 slices, soaked in hot water to soften
Salt	to taste

METHOD

- Heat oil in a deep pan or wok. Fry ginger, shallots, curry leaves and *halba campur* until shallots are browned.
- Add curry paste and continue to fry until oil separates to form a layer on top, then mix in salted fish and add coconut milk. Simmer for 10 minutes.
- Add pineapple and dried sour fruit. Simmer for another 10 minutes, then add salt to taste.
- Serve hot with plain steamed rice.

THAI FRIED PRAWNS WITH GARLIC

Note

The crisp-fried garlic in this recipe is an important and flavourful garnish. To make it at home, fry coarsely chopped peeled garlic in hot oil until golden brown, then drain on paper towels before using or storing. You will need to use about 250 ml (8 fl oz / 1 cup) oil for every 150 g (5 oz) of garlic. Crisp-fried garlic can be bought from certain supermarkets and Asian stores.

INGREDIENTS

Prawns (shrimps)	300 g (10 oz)
Cooking oil	80 ml (2½ fl oz)

MARINADE

Finely chopped garlic	2 Tbsp
Coriander (cilantro) roots	3–4
White peppercorns	1 Tbsp
Light soy sauce	2 Tbsp
Fish sauce	2 Tbsp
Sugar	a pinch or to taste

GARNISHING

Crisp-fried garlic (see note)	1 Tbsp
Coriander leaves (cilantro)	a few or to taste

METHOD

- With each prawn, trim off feelers and legs, then devein by making a slit from head to tail. Rinse clean and set aside until needed.

- Prepare marinade. Pound garlic, coriander roots and peppercorns together using a mortar and pestle until well-blended. Transfer mixture to a mixing bowl and add soy and fish sauces and sugar, if using. Mix in prawns and leave to marinate for 30 minutes.

- Heat oil in wok over medium-high heat. Stir-fry prawns briskly until they turn red, then dish out. Garnish as desired with crisp-fried garlic and coriander leaves. Serve immediately.

THAI DEEP-FRIED PRAWN TOAST

Note

Some wet markets may sell ready-minced prawn meat, but it is generally harder to find than minced fish meat (see pg 55). To mince prawn meat at home, either chop shelled and deveined prawns repeatedly with two cleavers or blend (process) it until it becomes a sticky paste. Sweet mango chutney or Thai sweet chilli sauce can be bought ready-made from most supermarkets and Asian stores.

INGREDIENTS

Minced prawn (shrimp) meat	200 g (7 oz)
Chopped coriander root	1 tsp
Light soy sauce	1 tsp
Egg	1, lightly beaten
Salt	to taste
Ground white pepper	to taste
Sliced white bread	8, toasted, crusts removed and cut into desired serving size pieces
White sesame seeds	2 Tbsp
Cooking oil for deep-frying	

METHOD

- Put prawn meat, coriander root, soy sauce and half the egg in a bowl and mix well. Season to taste with salt and pepper.
- Spread some prawn mixture evenly onto each slice of bread, then sprinkle sesame seeds over and press them in lightly.
- Heat sufficient oil for deep-frying. Quickly dip prawn paste side of bread slices in remaining egg; do not allow to soak. Add dipped bread slices to hot oil, prawn paste side down first, and deep-fry until golden brown on both sides. Drain well on paper towels.
- Serve immediately with sweet mango chutney or chilli sauce of choice.

SALMON WITH THAI RED CURRY SAUCE

INGREDIENTS

Salmon fillet	150 g (5 oz)
Cooking oil	1 Tbsp
Thai red curry paste	2 Tbsp
Kaffir lime leaves (*daun limau purut*)	2, central stems removed and finely sliced
Coconut cream (see pg 31)	250 ml (8 fl oz / 1 cup)
Water	125 ml (4 fl oz / ½ cup)
Dried prawns (shrimps) (*hae be*)	½ Tbsp, rinsed clean, soaked in water to soften, drained and finely pounded
Grated palm sugar (*gula Melaka*)	2 Tbsp
Fish sauce	2 tsp
Lime	½, squeezed for juice

GARNISHING

Thai sweet basil	1 small sprig
Red chilli strips	

METHOD

- Steam salmon for 4 minutes, then transfer to a serving dish. Set aside.

- Heat oil in a saucepan. Add curry paste and fry for 2 minutes or until fragrant.

- Add lime leaves, reserving some for garnishing, and coconut cream. Bring to the boil, then add water and simmer until sauce thickens.

- Add dried prawns, palm sugar, fish sauce and lime juice. Stir for 10 seconds or until sugar is completely dissolved. Adjust seasoning to taste, if necessary, and remove from heat.

- Pour sauce over salmon and garnish as desired with lime and basil leaves and chilli strips. Serve hot.

CRAB WITH BLACK PEPPER SAUCE

INGREDIENTS

Crab (any kind)	1, about 600 g (1 lb 5 oz), cleaned, top shell removed, pincers separated and body quartered
Plain (all-purpose) flour for dusting	
Cooking oil for deep-frying	
Salt	to taste

SPICE PASTE

Black peppercorns	15 g (½ oz)
Galangal (*lengkuas*)	10 g (⅓ oz), peeled and sliced
Lemon grass (*serai*)	2 stalks, sliced
Peeled onion	10 g (⅓ oz)
Garlic	1–2 cloves, peeled
Peeled shallots	10 g (⅓ oz)
Red chillies	4, seeded, if desired, and thickly sliced
Ginger	1–2 slices, peeled

METHOD

- Combine all spice paste ingredients in a blender (processor) until smooth. Set aside.
- Dust crab with flour and shake off excess. Heat sufficient oil for deep-frying in a deep pan or wok. Add crab pieces and fry until exposed flesh is lightly browned. Remove and drain on paper towels.
- Remove most of the oil to leave about 2 Tbsp behind. Reheat remaining oil over medium-low heat and fry spice paste until fragrant.
- Add fried crab pieces and stir-fry until they are well-coated with pan ingredients. Season to taste with salt, then dish out. Garnish and serve as desired.

RED SNAPPER TAGINE

Note

Tagine refers to both a Moroccan-style stew and a cooking utensil. A tagine dish is round with short sides and has a cone-shaped cover. A filled tagine dish is placed either in the oven or over stove-top heat, and the steam that rises from the food is trapped inside the cone. The moisture that collects there eventually returns to the food in a unique process that has been described as self-basting.

INGREDIENTS

Red snapper	1, about 1.5 kg (3 lb 4½ oz), cleaned
Canned plum (Roma) tomatoes	½ can, with juices, about 200 g (7 oz), crushed
Celery	1 stalk, chopped
Carrot	1, peeled, if desired, and chopped
Onion	1, peeled and chopped
Potatoes	2, peeled and sliced crossways
Red chilli	2, seeded, if desired, and chopped
Garlic	3 cloves, peeled
Black olives	10, pitted
Olive oil	125 ml (4 fl oz / ½ cup)
Salt	a pinch or more to taste
Fish stock	125 ml (4 fl oz / ½ cup), use ready-made (see pg 10) or home-made (see pg 13)
Lemons	1½, 1 cut into wedges and ½ squeezed for juice

SPICES

Paprika	2 Tbsp
Ground cumin (*jintan putih serbuk*)	1½ tsp
Saffron threads	a pinch
Freshly ground black pepper	to taste

HERBS

Freshly chopped parsley	a handful
Thyme	a handful
Mint leaves	a handful
Coriander leaves (cilantro)	a handful

METHOD

- Place fish in a tagine dish or casserole and rub in spices, then pour canned tomatoes and juices over.

- Arrange celery, carrot, onion, potatoes, chilli, garlic and olives along the sides. Reserve some herbs for garnishing and sprinkle the rest over. Drizzle olive oil on top and add salt to taste. Pour in fish stock.

- Cover with conical tagine cover or aluminium foil, if using a casserole. Bake in a preheated oven at 180°C (350°F) for 25 minutes or until fish is cooked.

- Remove from oven and sprinkle lemon juice over fish. Garnish as desired with reserved herbs and serve immediately, with lemon wedges on the side.

LEMON SOLE MEUNIÈRE
SOLE WITH LEMON BUTTER SAUCE

Note

The French cooking method known as meunière basically involves dusting fish fillets with flour and then frying them in butter. Meunière is similar to the Italian cooking method called piccata. Piccata, however, is also applied to meats such as veal, pork or chicken, not just fish.

INGREDIENTS

Sole fillets	2, about 300 g (10 oz)
Salt	to taste
Freshly ground black pepper	to taste
Plain (all-purpose) flour	1 Tbsp
Olive oil	2 Tbsp
Butter	3 Tbsp
White wine or fish stock	125 ml (4 fl oz / ½ cup), use ready-made (see pg 10) or home-made (see pg 13)
Lemon	1, ½ grated for zest and squeezed for juice, and remaining ½ sliced
Capers	1 Tbsp
Chopped parsley	a handful

METHOD

- Season fish with salt and pepper, then coat with flour and shake off excess.
- Heat olive oil and butter in a pan. Fry fish until golden brown on both sides and transfer to a serving dish when cooked.
- Add white wine or stock to pan to deglaze (see pg 14). When liquid is reduced by half, stir in lemon juice, capers and parsley. Spoon sauce over fish.
- Garnish as desired with lemon slices and zest. Serve immediately.

CRAB ENCHILADAS

Note

Enchiladas are a Mexican food that consist of tortillas wrapped around a filling, which can be meat- or seafood-based. They are served with a tomato-based sauce. Tortillas are a type of flat bread traditionally made from dried corn. Today, there is a variety of tortilla made from wheat flour. Corn tortillas can be found frozen in most supermarkets. Certain specialty stores may have freshly made ones.

INGREDIENTS

Cooking oil	4 Tbsp
Corn tortillas	6
Sour cream	to taste
Chopped almonds	2 Tbsp or to taste
Chopped fresh parsley	2 Tbsp or to taste

TOMATO SAUCE

Tomatoes	4, large, about 450 g (1 lb), peeled
Onion	½, medium, peeled
Garlic	1 clove, peeled
Jalapeño chilli	1 or to taste
Cooking oil	1 Tbsp
Salt	½ tsp or to taste

FILLING

Cooking oil	1 Tbsp
Onion	½, medium, peeled and chopped
Garlic	1 clove, peeled and chopped
Cooked or canned crab meat	170 g (5½ oz), drained and flaked
Green olives	3, pitted and chopped
Raisins	1 Tbsp, soaked in hot water to plump up and drained
Chopped almonds	1 Tbsp
Chopped parsley	1 Tbsp
Capers	1 tsp
Salt	to taste

METHOD

- Prepare tomato sauce. Combine all ingredients, except oil and salt, in a blender (processor) until smooth. Heat oil in a medium saucepan, then add blended mixture and salt to taste. Bring to the boil, reduce heat and simmer gently, uncovered, for 10 minutes; you should get about 500 ml (16 fl oz / 2 cups) of sauce. Keep warm.

- Prepare filling. Heat oil in a pan over medium-low heat. Add onion and garlic and cook until transparent and softened. Add all remaining ingredients, including salt to taste. Stir for about 5 minutes until well-mixed. Remove from heat.

- Heat 4 Tbsp oil in a medium pan. Use tongs to lower tortillas, one at a time, into hot oil. Fry until lightly browned on both sides. Drain on paper towels.

- Spoon a portion of filling onto each tortilla and wrap up by folding in left and right sides, then place them in a baking dish. Spoon tomato sauce over all the wraps and cover baking dish with aluminium foil.

- Bake in a preheated oven at 180°C (350°F) for about 15 minutes or until heated through.

- Carefully transfer enchiladas to individual serving plates. Add desired amount of sour cream and sprinkle with almonds and parsley. Serve immediately.

FISH CEVICHE

Note

Ceviche is a dish of raw fish marinated in lime or lemon juice and mixed with any number of complementary ingredients. In South America, where this dish originated, preparations of ceviche vary from country to country, even household to household. Peru, Ecuador, Chile and Mexico all have their distinctive versions. Feel free to add to or subtract from the list of complementary ingredients in this recipe to suit your own or your family's tastes.

INGREDIENTS

Spanish mackerel (*ikan tenggiri*) meat	300 g (10 oz), diced
Limes (*limau nipis*)	8, squeezed for juice
Freshly cracked black pepper	to taste
Salt	to taste
Sugar	a pinch
Olive oil	4 Tbsp
Red onion	1, peeled and chopped
Tomatoes	2, chopped
Avocado	1, peeled, stoned and chopped
Red chilli	1, seeded, if desired, and chopped
Green chilli	1, seeded, if desired, and chopped
Pineapple	¼, peeled and chopped
Coriander leaves (cilantro)	1 sprig, chopped
Spring onions (scallions)	1–2, chopped

GARNISHING

Parsley	1 small sprig
Red chilli	1, seeded and finely chopped

METHOD

- Put fish into a large bowl and mix with lime juice. Cover with plastic wrap and refrigerate for at least 1 hour. Fish should have changed to a whitish colour and look 'cooked' at the end of refrigeration.

- Add all remaining ingredients and mix well. Adjust seasoning to taste with more salt, sugar or lime juice, then transfer to a serving dish or divide into individual portions to serve.

- Garnish as desired with parsley and red chilli and serve immediately.

GOAN-INSPIRED FISH CURRY

Note

Goan fish curry is typically yellow in colour because of the presence of turmeric and quite chunky with tomato wedges and thickly sliced chillies. This recipe is my interpretation of the Goan fish curry. While a little unorthodox, it does produce an exceptionally flavourful gravy that is best enjoyed with a serving of plain, steamed rice. The chilli paste, better known as cili boh, can be store-bought or made by blending pre-soaked dried chillies until smooth.

INGREDIENTS

Tomatoes	3, cut into wedges
Green chillies	3, seeded, if desired, and sliced
Cooking oil	250 ml (8 fl oz / 1 cup)
Onions	2, peeled and chopped
Garlic	3 cloves, peeled and minced
Ginger	2-cm (1-in) knob, peeled and minced
Black mustard seeds	2 Tbsp
Chilli paste (*cili boh*) (see note)	4 Tbsp
Coconut cream (see pg 31)	500 ml (16 fl oz / 2 cups)
Tamarind (*asam Jawa*) juice (see pg 32)	125 ml (4 fl oz / ½ cup)
Spanish mackerel (*ikan tenggiri*) steaks	600 g (1 lb 5 oz), 4–5 steaks, cleaned
Salt	to taste
Curry leaves	1 sprig

DRY SPICES

Ground coriander (*ketumbar serbuk*)	3 Tbsp
Ground cumin (*jintan putih serbuk*)	3 tsp
Ground turmeric (*kunyit serbuk*)	2 tsp

METHOD

- Combine tomatoes, chillies and dry spices in a blender (processor) until smooth. Set aside.
- Heat oil in a pot over medium-low heat. Fry onions, garlic, ginger and mustard seeds until golden and fragrant.
- Add blended mixture, chilli paste and coconut cream. Stir to mix well, then bring to the boil and simmer for 2 minutes. Thin gravy down with a little water, if too thick.
- Add tamarind juice and fish steaks. Stir through and simmer for 15 minutes or until fish is cooked. Season to taste with salt.
- Dish out, garnish as desired with curry leaves and serve.

FISH-STUFFED BITTER GOURD

INGREDIENTS

Bitter gourd	500 g (1 lb 1½ oz), cut into 2-cm (1-in) rings, seeded and white pith removed
Corn flour (cornstarch)	3 Tbsp
Minced fish meat (see pg 55)	450 g (1 lb)
Cooking oil	4 Tbsp
Water	875 ml (29 fl oz / 3½ cups)
Coconut cream (see pg 31)	250 ml (8 fl oz / 1 cup)

SPICE PASTE

Onions	2, peeled
Garlic	2 cloves, peeled
Galangal (*lengkuas*)	2.5-cm (1-in) knob, peeled
White peppercorns	15
Candlenuts (*buah keras*)	3
Lemon grass (*serai*)	2 stalks, sliced
Dried prawn (shrimp) paste	1½ tsp
Turmeric (*kunyit*)	2.5-cm (1-in) knob, peeled

SEASONING

Salt	1½ tsp or to taste
Sugar	2 tsp or to taste
Anchovy (*ikan bilis*) stock granules (optional)	1 tsp

METHOD

- Blanch bitter gourd pieces: lower them into boiling water for 5 minutes, then drain and plunge into cold water for 5 minutes to refresh. Drain using a colander and set aside. Blanching enhances the colour and flavour of the ingredient.

- Combine all spice paste ingredients in a blender (processor) until smooth. Set aside.

- Dust insides of bitter gourd pieces with corn flour, then stuff with fish meat and place on a greased plate.

- Heat oil in a pan and fry spice paste over medium-low heat until fragrant. Add water and simmer for 12–15 minutes.

- Add seasoning ingredients and stuffed bitter gourd pieces. Gently stir through and simmer until fish meat is cooked: it turns white.

- Add coconut cream and bring to the boil, then switch off heat and dish out to serve.

SPICY PRAWN AND PUMPKIN GULAI

Note

Some cooks like this dish to have a pronounced tartness, so they make the tamarind juice for this recipe really thick and concentrated.

INGREDIENTS

Ghee (clarified butter)	4 Tbsp
Onion	1, peeled and finely diced
Ginger	2-cm (1-in) knob, peeled and thinly sliced
Garlic	2 cloves, peeled and finely chopped
Pumpkin	750 g (1 lb 5 oz), peeled, seeded, pith removed and thickly sliced
Fish curry powder	4 Tbsp
Chilli powder (optional)	1 Tbsp
Water	500 ml (16 fl oz / 2 cups)
Salt	a pinch or to taste
Shelled prawns (shrimps)	200 g (7 oz), deveined
Brown sugar	2 Tbsp
Tamarind (*asam Jawa*) juice (see pg 32)	4 Tbsp
Coriander leaves (cilantro)	a handful

SPICES

Fenugreek seeds (*halba*)	1 Tbsp
Cumin seeds (*jintan putih biji*)	1 tsp
Cinnamon (*kayu manis*)	1-cm (½-in) piece

METHOD

- Heat ghee over medium-low heat. Fry onion, ginger, garlic and spices until fragrant.
- Add pumpkin, curry powder and chilli powder, if using, and stir-fry until well-mixed.
- Add water and salt to taste, then simmer until pumpkin is cooked. Add a little hot water, if dry.
- Add prawns, brown sugar, tamarind juice and coriander leaves, reserving some for garnishing. Continue to simmer until gravy is thick. Adjust seasoning to taste with more salt or sugar, if necessary, then dish out.
- Garnish as desired with coriander leaves and serve warm.

GULAI ASAM REBUS KELADI
TANGY YAM AND PRAWN CURRY

INGREDIENTS

Yam (taro)	1 kg (2 lb 3 oz), peeled and cut into bite-size pieces
Water	2 litres (64 fl oz / 8 cups)
Dried sour fruit (*asam gelugur*)	3 slices
Shelled prawns (shrimps)	300 g (10 oz), deveined
Salt	to taste
Sugar	to taste
Polygonum (*laksa*) leaves (see pg 42)	a bunch

SPICE PASTE

Red chillies	10, seeded, if desired, and thickly sliced
Bird's eye chillies (*cili padi*)	6
Garlic	2 cloves, peeled
Shallots	15, peeled
Dried prawn (shrimp) paste (*belacan*)	1-cm (½-in) piece, dry-roasted (see pg 22)

METHOD

- Combine all spice paste ingredients in a blender (processor) until smooth, then pour into a pot.
- Add yam, water and dried sour fruit to the pot and bring to the boil over medium heat. Reduce heat to low and simmer, stirring regularly, for about 20 minutes or until yam is tender.
- Add prawns and season to taste with salt and sugar. Simmer for about 5 minutes or until prawns are cooked.
- Lastly, add polygonum leaves and stir through, then dish out and serve warm with plain rice.

SPANISH MACKEREL IN SOY BEAN PASTE

INGREDIENTS

Spanish mackerel (*ikan tenggiri*) steaks	400 g (13½ oz), 3–4 steaks
Cooking oil	2 Tbsp + enough for shallow-frying
Garlic	4 cloves, peeled and minced
Ginger	2-cm (1-in) knob, peeled and minced
Preserved soy bean paste (*taucu*)	4 Tbsp
Chilli paste (*cili boh*) (see pg 85)	1 Tbsp
Oyster sauce	2 Tbsp
Chinese cooking wine (*hua tiao*) or chicken stock (see pg 16)	4 Tbsp
Aubergine (eggplant/brinjal)	1, ends trimmed off and cut into large cubes
Red capsicum (bell pepper)	1, seeded, white pith removed and cut into large squares
Coriander leaves (cilantro)	a bunch
Spring onions (scallions)	4, sliced
Salt	to taste
Sugar	to taste

METHOD

- Shallow-fry fish steaks in hot oil until cooked and golden brown on both sides. Drain on paper towels.
- Heat 2 Tbsp oil in a pan over medium heat. Fry garlic, ginger and soy bean and chilli pastes for 2 minutes.
- Add oyster sauce, wine or stock and fried fish. Stir-fry gently to coat fish with pan ingredients; do not be too vigorous or the fish steaks will break.
- Add aubergine, capsicum, coriander leaves and spring onions. Stir-fry gently to mix well, then season to taste with salt and sugar. Dish out and serve immediately.

STEAMED GROUPER WITH MANGO

INGREDIENTS

Grouper	1, about 1.5–2 kg (3 lb 4½ oz–4 lb 6 oz), cleaned
Salt	a pinch
Garlic	2 cloves, peeled and finely chopped
Ginger	2-cm (1-in) knob, peeled and sliced
Galangal (*lengkuas*)	2-cm (1-in) knob, peeled and sliced
Tomatoes	2, cut into wedges
Ripe mango	1, peeled, seeded and sliced into strips
Bird's eye chillies (*cili padi*)	6, seeded, if desired, and halved
Kaffir lime leaves (*daun limau purut*)	3, central stems removed and shredded
Lemon grass (*serai*)	2 stalks, thinly sliced
Lime (*limau nipis*)	1, squeezed for juice

GARNISHING

Coriander leaves (cilantro)	a handful
Spring onion (scallion)	1, use green part only, shredded and soaked in ice water to make them curl

METHOD

- Season fish with salt, then place on a steaming plate. Add all remaining ingredients, except garnishing ingredients, arranging as desired over and around fish.

- Steam for 20 minutes or until fish is cooked. Garnish as desired with coriander leaves and spring onion. Serve immediately.

CORN AND PRAWN FRITTERS

INGREDIENTS

Yellow lentils	150 g (5 oz), rinsed clean
Cooking oil	125 ml (4 fl oz / ½ cup) + for deep-frying
Dried prawns (shrimps) (*hae be*)	75 g (2½ oz / ½ cup), rinsed clean, soaked in water to soften and drained
Plain (all-purpose) flour	300 g (10 oz)
Baking powder	2 tsp
Ground turmeric (*kunyit serbuk*)	1 tsp
Canned cream corn	1 can, about 410 g (13½ oz)
Shelled prawns (shrimps)	200 g (7 oz), deveined
Eggs	2, beaten
Onion	1, large, peeled and chopped
Tomato	1, diced
Bean sprouts	150 g (5 oz), tailed, if desired
Green chillies	2, seeded, if desired, and minced
Sliced Chinese chives (*ku cai*)	a handful

METHOD

- Boil lentils in water for 10–15 minutes or until tender, then drain and place under running water to cool. Set aside to drain well.
- Heat 125 ml (4 fl oz / ½ cup) oil in a small pot. Dry dried prawns with paper towels and add to hot oil to fry until golden brown and crisp. Remove and drain on paper towels, then finely pound.
- Put cooked lentils and pounded dried prawns in a large bowl. Add all remaining ingredients and mix well into a batter.
- Heat sufficient oil for deep-frying. Drop spoonfuls of batter into hot oil and deep-fry until golden. Drain on paper towels and serve warm with dipping sauce of your choice.

POULTRY

THAI GREEN CHICKEN CURRY

INGREDIENTS

Cooking oil	2 Tbsp
Thai green curry paste	4 Tbsp
Coconut milk (see pg 60)	500 ml (16 fl oz / 2 cups)
Chicken breast or thigh meat	150 g (5 oz), cut into bite-size pieces
Thai aubergines (eggplants/brinjals)	4, ends trimmed and quartered
Pea aubergines	20, rinsed clean
Fish sauce	2 Tbsp
Sugar	2 tsp
Kaffir lime leaves (*daun limau purut*)	4, torn in half
Green chillies	2, seeded, if desired, and thinly sliced
Thai sweet basil leaves	20

SPICES

Cumin seeds (*jintan putih biji*)	½ tsp
Coriander seeds (*ketumbar biji*)	½ tsp

GARNISHING (OPTIONAL)

Coconut cream (see pg 31)	2 Tbsp
Coriander leaves (cilantro) (optional)	2 sprigs

METHOD

- Dry-roast spices: put them into a dry pan placed over low heat and stir until fragrant. If preferred, transfer to a mortar and finely grind with a pestle. Otherwise, use whole.

- Heat oil in a saucepan or pot. Add curry paste and spices. Stir-fry over medium heat until fragrant. Reduce heat and add coconut milk, a little at a time, stirring to mix well after each addition. When all of it has been added, bring to the boil and simmer for 1 minute.

- Add chicken and both aubergines. Simmer for about 10 minutes or until chicken is cooked, then add fish sauce, sugar, lime leaves and chillies. Simmer for 5 minutes more.

- Add basil leaves and stir through, then transfer to a serving dish or bowl. Garnish, if using, as desired with coconut cream and coriander leaves. Serve warm with plain rice.

STIR-FRIED CHICKEN WITH CASHEW NUTS

INGREDIENTS

Cooking oil	4 Tbsp
Dried chillies	6, rinsed clean, soaked in water to soften and cut into bite-size pieces
Cashew nuts	200 g (7 oz)
Sesame oil	2 Tbsp
Finely chopped garlic	4 tsp
Chicken breast or thigh meat	400 g (13½ oz), cut into bite-size pieces
Onion	½, medium, peeled and diced
Cored pineapple	50 g (2 oz), diced
Green capsicum (bell pepper)	1, small, seeded, white pith removed and cut into bite-size pieces
Tomato sauce (ketchup)	250 ml (8 fl oz / 1 cup)
Chilli sauce	90 ml (3 fl oz / 6 Tbsp)
Light soy sauce	2 tsp
Sugar	2 Tbsp or to taste
Salt	½ tsp or to taste

METHOD

- Heat cooking oil in a pan. Fry dried chillies and cashew nuts until cashew nuts are golden brown, then remove pan from heat. Transfer fried ingredients to a plate and set aside.

- Add sesame oil to pan and mix oils together, then reheat over medium heat. Add garlic and stir-fry until fragrant.

- Add chicken and stir-fry briskly for 1 minute before adding onion, pineapple and capsicum. Continue to stir-fry until chicken is cooked.

- Add tomato, chilli and soy sauces, then adjust seasoning to taste. Add sugar and salt to taste.

- Finally, add fried dried chillies and cashew nuts. Stir-fry until well-mixed, then dish out. Garnish and serve as desired.

CHICKEN AND PINEAPPLE STIR-FRY

INGREDIENTS

Cooking oil	4 Tbsp
Chicken breast or thigh meat	500 g (1 lb 1½ oz), cut into large cubes
Lemon grass (*serai*)	1 stalk, bruised
Onion	1, peeled and cut into wedges
Tomatoes	2, cut into wedges
Pineapple	¼, peeled, cored and cut into bite-size pieces
Red and green chillies	1 each, diagonally sliced
Kaffir lime leaves (*daun limau purut*)	2, torn or bruised
Oyster sauce	1 Tbsp
Fish sauce	1 Tbsp
Sugar	to taste
Salt	to taste

SPICE PASTE

Dried prawns (shrimps)	4 Tbsp, rinsed clean, soaked in water to soften and drained
Dried prawn (shrimp) paste (*belacan*)	1 Tbsp, dry-roasted (see pg 22)
Chilli paste (*cili boh*) (see pg 85)	3 Tbsp
Shallots	5, peeled
Garlic	2 cloves, peeled
Coriander roots	2

METHOD

- Combine all spice paste ingredients in a blender (processor) until smooth. Set aside.
- Heat 1 Tbsp oil in a deep pan or wok. Fry chicken until lightly browned. Remove and set aside.
- Add remaining oil to pan and reheat over low heat. Fry spice paste with lemon grass until fragrant.
- Add onion, tomatoes, pineapple, chillies, lime leaves and chicken. Stir-fry until well-mixed, then add oyster and fish sauces. Adjust seasoning to taste with sugar and salt to taste, if necessary.
- Increase heat to medium and cook, covered, for 3 minutes. Dish out and serve as desired.

THAI PANDAN CHICKEN

Note

The marinated chicken in this recipe can be wrapped in different ways. Many Thai restaurants serve them fashioned into decorative parcels, which can be complicated to prepare. The key, however, is to enclose the chicken pieces sufficiently so they do not fall out during frying, and also absorb some fragrance of screwpine leaves. Thus, wrap chicken in whatever way is most manageable for you. See method for a few suggestions.

INGREDIENTS

Chicken breast or thigh meat	350 g (12 oz), cut into small chunks, approximately 2.5-cm (1-in) cubes
Screwpine (*pandan*) leaves	10–12, large, rinsed clean
Cooking oil for deep-frying	

MARINADE

Minced garlic	1 Tbsp
Whipping cream	1 Tbsp
Milk	1 Tbsp
Chilli sauce	2 Tbsp
Oyster sauce	1 Tbsp
Dark soy sauce	1 Tbsp
Sesame oil	1 Tbsp
Sugar	2 tsp
Ground white pepper	2 tsp

SAUCE

Grated palm sugar (*gula Melaka*)	160 g (5½ oz / 1 cup), melted
Vinegar	125 ml (4 fl oz / ½ cup)
Dark soy sauce	1 tsp
Minced ginger	1½ tsp
White sesame seeds	1 Tbsp, dry-roasted (see pg 35)

METHOD

- Combine all marinade ingredients in a bowl and stir to blend. Mix in chicken and refrigerate for at least 1 hour to marinate.
- Meanwhile, prepare sauce. Mix together all ingredients, except sesame seeds, in a bowl. Stir to blend, then adjust to taste with more sugar or vinegar. Set aside.
- Wrap marinated chicken with screwpine leaves. One method is to place 3–4 pieces of chicken about 7.5 cm (3 in) from the short end of a leaf, then fold leaf over to cover chicken and secure tightly with a cocktail stick. Trim off excess leaf and use it to wrap the chicken again so the exposed sides are also covered. Weave one end of the leaf through the existing loop and secure with another cocktail stick.
- Alternatively, wrap 1–2 pieces of chicken with a squarish piece of screwpine leaf. First, place the chicken on the centre of the leaf square, then lift all four corners over the chicken and secure with a cocktail stick or by stapling.
- Still one more method is to place 2–3 pieces of chicken along the short end of a screwpine leaf and roll up tightly several rounds so it resembles a sushi roll. Secure with a cocktail stick, then trim off excess leaf and repeat with remaining chicken.
- When all the chicken has been wrapped, heat sufficient oil for deep-frying. Add parcels, a few at a time, to hot oil and fry each batch until cooked; 3–4 minutes for larger parcels and 2 minutes for smaller parcels. Drain in a sieve or colander, then on paper towels, if preferred.
- Sprinkle sesame seeds over prepared sauce and serve with well drained chicken parcels.

CHICKEN TIKKA

Note

Tikka *is the Hindi word for chunks of meat that have been marinated in yoghurt and spices, and roasted—quite similar to kebabs.*

INGREDIENTS

Chicken	1, about 1.2 kg (2 lb 10 oz), skinned and boned, or 450 g (1 lb) chicken breast or thigh meat
Grated ginger	2 tsp
Grated garlic	2 tsp
Yoghurt	4 Tbsp
Lime (*limau nipis*) juice	2 tsp
Salt	to taste
Butter or corn oil for basting	

DRY SPICES

Chilli powder	1 tsp
Ground turmeric (*kunyit serbuk*)	½ tsp
Garam masala	¼ tsp
Ground white pepper	¼ tsp

GARNISHING

Lemon wedges

Raw onion rings

METHOD

- Remove excess fat from chicken meat and cut into 4-cm (2-in) cubes. Set aside.
- Put ginger and garlic in a bowl. Add dry spices, yoghurt, lime juice and salt to taste. Mix together into a smooth, thick paste. Adjust seasoning to taste with more salt, lime juice or spices as preferred.
- Mix in chicken pieces and leave to marinate for at least 4 hours, or preferably overnight, in the refrigerator.
- Thread marinated chicken onto skewers, leaving 5-cm (2-in) gaps between pieces.
- Roast chicken in a preheated oven at 200°C (400°F) for 10–15 minutes, basting with butter or corn oil and turning over once.
- When chicken is cooked, remove from oven and allow to rest for 5 minutes before serving. If preferred, take chicken pieces off cooking skewers and thread onto trimmed lemon grass stalks.
- Place chicken onto a large serving dish or divide among individual serving ones. Garnish as desired with lemon wedges and onion rings and serve.

CHICKEN BAMIA

Note

Bamia *is Middle Eastern in origin and several variations exist in the world today. This dish, like many others, adapted to local tastes as it spread from place to place. This recipe, in particular, reflects Malay influence with the addition of evaporated milk, which makes the sauce much richer than that of the original. This recipe also avoids the traditional way of cooking ladies' fingers—stewing them until they are sappy and sticky.*

INGREDIENTS

Ghee (clarified butter)	125 ml (4 fl oz / ½ cup)
Almonds	15, with skins intact
Screwpine (*pandan*) leaves	2, washed, shredded and knotted
Chicken	1, about 1.2 kg (2 lb 10 oz), cut into 8 pieces
Meat curry powder	3 Tbsp
Tomatoes	4, peeled and crushed
Green chillies	3, sliced
Water	750 ml (24 fl oz / 3 cups)
Carrots	2, peeled, if desired, and sliced
Tomato paste	2 Tbsp
Evaporated milk	125 ml (4 fl oz / ½ cup)
Ladies' fingers (okra)	15, diagonally sliced into bite-size pieces
Salt	to taste
Sugar	to taste
Lemon juice	1 Tbsp
Coriander leaves (cilantro)	a handful, chopped + extra for garnishing

SPICES

Cloves (*bunga cengkih*)	3 or to taste
Cardamoms (*bunga pelaga*)	4 pods
Cinnamon (*kayu manis*)	5-cm (2-in) stick or to taste

SPICE PASTE

Shallots	10, peeled
Garlic	6 cloves, peeled
Ginger	2-cm (1-in) knob, peeled
Onion	1, peeled

METHOD

- Combine all spice paste ingredients in a blender (processor) until smooth.

- Heat ghee in a large pan and fry spice paste, spices, almonds and screwpine leaves over medium-low heat until fragrant.

- Add chicken and curry powder. Stir-fry for 5 minutes until chicken is well-coated with pan ingredients.

- Add tomatoes and chillies. Reduce heat to low and cook, stirring occasionally, until juices from tomatoes dry up.

- Add water and carrots, then simmer for 25 minutes or until chicken is tender.

- Add tomato paste, milk and ladies' fingers and cook until sauce thickens, about 10 minutes.

- Season to taste with salt and sugar, then stir in lemon juice and coriander.

- Dish out and garnish as desired with extra coriander leaves. Serve warm.

SRI LANKAN PEPPER CHICKEN

INGREDIENTS

Chicken	8 pieces, each about 7.5 x 5 cm (3 x 2 in)
Potato wedges	2, thick
Cooking oil for shallow- or deep-frying	
Ghee (clarified butter)	4 Tbsp
Onions	2, peeled and finely chopped
Garlic	4 cloves, peeled and finely chopped
Ginger	2-cm (1-in) knob, peeled and chopped
Curry leaves	4
Yoghurt	250 ml (8 fl oz / 1 cup)
Tomato sauce (ketchup)	3 Tbsp
Tomatoes	2, cut into wedges
Cashew nuts	70 g (2½ oz / ½ cup), dry-roasted until golden (see pg 35)

DRY SPICES

Black peppercorns	1 Tbsp, crushed
Chilli powder	1 tsp
Ground turmeric (*kunyit serbuk*)	1 tsp
Ground cumin (*jintan putih serbuk*)	1 tsp
Ground cloves (*bunga cengkih serbuk*)	½ tsp

METHOD

- Shallow- or deep-fry chicken, then potato wedges, in hot oil until golden brown. Drain on paper towels.
- Heat ghee in a pan. Add onions, garlic, ginger and curry leaves. Fry over low heat until aromatic and garlic is golden.
- Add dry spices and stir for about 1 minute, then add yoghurt and tomato sauce. Cook, stirring constantly, until slightly thickened. Stir in a little water, if mixture is too thick and sticking to the pan.
- Add fried chicken pieces and stir until they are well-coated with pan ingredients before adding potato wedges, tomatoes and cashew nuts. Stir for 1–2 minutes more, then dish out and serve.

CHICKEN AND VEGETABLE DHALCA

INGREDIENTS

Cooking oil	4 Tbsp
Shallots	15, peeled and minced
Garlic	3 cloves, peeled and minced
Ginger	2.5-cm (1-in) knob, peeled and minced
Curry leaves	4
Meat curry powder	6 Tbsp
Chilli powder (optional)	1 Tbsp
Chicken breast or thigh meat	300 g (10 oz), cut into bite-size pieces
Yellow lentils	200 g (7 oz), rinsed clean and parboiled for 7–10 minutes
Carrot	1, peeled, if desired, and cut into bite-size pieces
Potatoes	2, peeled and cut into bite-size pieces
Long (snake) beans	150 g (5 oz), cut to 3-cm (1½-in) lengths
Coconut cream (see pg 31)	250 ml (8 fl oz / 1 cup)
Aubergine (eggplant/brinjal)	1, ends trimmed and cut into bite-size pieces
Courgette (zucchini)	1, ends trimmed and cut into bite-size pieces
Ladies' fingers (okra)	10, halved crossways
Tomatoes	3, cut into wedges
Tamarind (*asam Jawa*) juice (see pg 32)	125 ml (4 fl oz / ½ cup)
Salt	to taste
Sugar	to taste

SPICES

Star anise (*bunga lawang*)	3 points or to taste
Cloves (*bunga cengkih*)	4 or to taste
Cinnamon (*kayu manis*)	2-cm (1-in) stick
Cardamoms (*buah pelaga*)	4 pods

METHOD

- Heat oil in a pot over medium-low heat. Fry shallots, garlic, ginger and spices until a little browned.

- Add curry leaves and powder, chilli powder, if using, and chicken. Fry until aromatic and chicken changes colour. Add a little water to prevent sticking, if necessary.

- Add lentils and enough water to cover ingredients. Stir through, then add carrot, potatoes and long beans. Add more water to just immerse vegetables, if necessary. Bring to the boil and simmer for 10 minutes, stirring regularly.

- Add coconut cream, aubergine, courgette, ladies' fingers, tomatoes and tamarind juice. Stir through and simmer until vegetables are tender or done to your liking. Season to taste with salt and sugar.

- Dish out, then garnish and serve as desired.

TANGY AND SPICY
FRIED CHICKEN

Note

For added flavour, season chicken pieces with a pinch each of salt and ground turmeric, and 1 Tbsp oyster sauce before frying until cooked.

INGREDIENTS

Chicken	8 pieces, each about 7.5 x 5 cm (3 x 2 in)
Cooking oil	8 Tbsp + enough for shallow- or deep-frying
Aubergines (eggplants/brinjals)	2, ends trimmed and diced
Tamarind (*asam Jawa*) juice (see pg 32)	125 ml (4 fl oz / ½ cup)
Lemon grass (*serai*)	1 stalk, bruised
Pineapple	½, peeled and diced
Salt	to taste
Sugar	to taste
Polygonum (*laksa*) leaves (see pg 42)	a handful

SPICE PASTE

Red chillies	10
Garlic	3, cloves, peeled
Young ginger	2-cm (1-in) knob, peeled
Turmeric (*kunyit*)	1-cm (½-in) knob, peeled
Torch ginger bud (*bunga kantan*)	½, sliced + extra for garnishing
Kaffir lime leaves (*daun limau purut*)	2, central stems removed
Dried prawn (shrimp) paste (*belacan*)	2 tsp, dry-roasted (see pg 22)

METHOD

- Shallow- or deep-fry chicken in hot oil until golden and drain on paper towels. Set aside.
- Heat 4 Tbsp oil in a pan and fry aubergines until just cooked. Drain on paper towels and set aside.
- Combine all spice paste ingredients in a blender (processor) and pulse several times to chop coarsely. Do not purée; you want some texture in the mixture.
- Heat remaining oil in a pan and fry spice paste over medium-low heat until fragrant. Add fried chicken, tamarind juice, lemon grass and pineapple. Cook, stirring regularly, until sauce thickens.
- Season to taste with salt and sugar. Add fried aubergines and polygonum leaves. Stir through.
- Dish out and garnish as desired with extra torch ginger bud. Serve warm with rice.

CHICKEN RENDANG
MALAY CURRIED CHICKEN STEW

Note

Blimbing is a small, tropical fruit that is lime green in colour and typically grows to about 4-cm (2-in) long. It imparts sourness to a dish and belongs to the same botanical family as star fruit. If unavailable, replace with lime or lemon juice to taste. Fresh lesser galangal can be hard to find outside of Asia, but Asian stores are likely to sell either the frozen or dried form. Use the ground variety only as a last resort and sparingly, 1 tsp at a time.

INGREDIENTS

Cooking oil	4 Tbsp
Chicken joints	500 g (1 lb 1½ oz)
Black peppercorns	1 tsp or to taste, coarsely pounded
Lemon grass (*serai*)	2 stalks, bruised
Kaffir lime leaves (*daun limau purut*)	3, torn or bruised
Dried sour fruit (*asam gelugur*)	2 pieces
Coconut cream (see pg 31)	250 ml (8 fl oz / 1 cup)
Water	250 ml (8 fl oz / 1 cup)
Kerisik (see pg 26)	3 Tbsp
Palm sugar (*gula Melaka*)	1 Tbsp
Salt	to taste
Blimbing (*belimbing*)	2–3
Basil leaves	1 sprig

SPICE PASTE

Garlic	10 cloves, peeled
Shallots	8, peeled
Bird's eye chillies (*cili padi*)	15
Dried chillies	6, rinsed clean, soaked in water to soften and drained
Ginger	10 g (⅓ oz), peeled and sliced
Turmeric (*kunyit*)	10 g (⅓ oz), peeled and sliced
Galangal (*lengkuas*)	10 g (⅓ oz), peeled and sliced
Lesser galangal (*cekur* or *kencur*)	1 piece, peeled and thickly sliced

METHOD

- Combine all spice paste ingredients in a blender (processor) until smooth.

- Heat oil in a deep pan or pot. Fry spice paste over low heat until fragrant and oil separates to form a layer on top.

- Add chicken pieces and stir until they are well-coated with pan ingredients, then add black peppercorns, lemon grass, lime leaves, dried sour fruit, coconut cream and water. Stir through and simmer, stirring frequently, until chicken is cooked.

- Add *kerisik*, palm sugar and salt to taste. Continue to simmer and stir frequently until gravy is thick and clings to the chicken.

- Add blimbing and basil leaves. Stir through and cook for 2–3 minutes more, then dish out and serve warm.

AYAM PERCIK
GRILLED CHICKEN IN SPICY GRAVY

INGREDIENTS

Coconut milk (see pg 60)	1 litre (32 fl oz / 4 cups)
Chicken	1, about 1 kg (2 lb 3 oz), cleaned and halved lengthways
Lemon grass (*serai*)	10 stalks, bruised
Galangal (*lengkuas*)	6-cm (2½-in) knob, peeled, thickly sliced and bruised
Salt	a pinch or to taste
Sugar	a pinch or to taste
Turmeric leaf (*daun kunyit*)	½, finely sliced

SPICE PASTE

Red chillies	3, seeded, if desired
Shallots	4, peeled
Garlic	3 cloves, peeled
Ginger	2.5-cm (1-in) knob, peeled
Turmeric (*kunyit*)	2.5-cm (1-in) knob, peeled
Candlenuts (*buah keras*)	10
Fenugreek seeds (*halba*)	1 tsp

METHOD

- Combine all spice paste ingredients in a blender (processor) until smooth. Transfer to a large pot.
- Add coconut milk to spice paste. Stir through and bring to the boil, then simmer until oil separates to form a layer on top.
- Add chicken, lemon grass and galangal. Stir until chicken is well-coated with pan ingredients, then season to taste with salt and sugar. Simmer for 30 minutes, stirring and turning regularly. Add a little water to prevent sticking, if dry, but liquid level in the pot should always be as low as possible.
- Remove chicken from gravy and charcoal- or oven-grill it for 10 minutes, basting frequently with gravy from the pot. Place grilled chicken on a serving plate.
- Return pot to the stove and reduce remaining gravy over medium-low heat, stirring constantly, until it thickens further to the point where it will cling to the chicken when spooned over.
- When gravy is ready, remove from heat and spoon over chicken. Garnish as desired with turmeric leaves and serve immediately.

OPOR CHICKEN WITH YAM

INGREDIENTS

Cooking oil	4 Tbsp
Shallots	4, peeled and thinly sliced
Garlic	2 cloves, peeled and thinly sliced
Kaffir lime leaves (*daun limau purut*)	3, torn or bruised
Lemon grass (*serai*)	2 stalks, bruised
Chicken	500 g (1 lb 1½ oz), cleaned and cut into joints
Coconut milk (see pg 60)	250 ml (8 fl oz / 1 cup)
Kerisik (see pg 26)	2 Tbsp
Salt	to taste
Yam (taro)	300 g (10 oz), peeled and cut into bite-size pieces
Red chillies	3, halved lengthways and seeded, if desired
Green chillies	3, halved lengthways and seeded, if desired

SPICE PASTE

Ginger	10 g (⅓ oz), peeled and thickly sliced
Galangal (*lengkuas*)	10 g (⅓ oz), peeled and thickly sliced
Bird's eye chillies (*cili padi*)	8
Candlenuts (*buah keras*)	4

WHOLE SPICES

Cloves (*bunga cengkih*)	4 or to taste
Cardamoms (*bunga pelaga*)	4 pods or to taste
Cinnamon (*kayu manis*)	3-cm (1½-in) stick

DRY SPICES

Ground fennel (*jintan manis serbuk*)	1 Tbsp
Ground cumin (*jintan putih serbuk*)	1 Tbsp
Ground turmeric (*kunyit serbuk*)	½ tsp
Ground coriander (*ketumbar serbuk*)	1 tsp

METHOD

- Combine all spice paste ingredients in a blender (processor) until fine. Set aside.
- Heat oil in a deep pan or pot. Fry shallots, garlic and whole spices over medium-low heat until shallots and garlic are browned. Add oil as necessary.
- Add lime leaves, lemon grass, spice paste and dry spices. Stir constantly until mixture is fragrant. Add a little water to prevent sticking, if necessary.
- Add chicken pieces and stir until they are well-coated with pan ingredients, then cook until flavours from the spices have penetrated the meat.
- Add coconut milk, *kerisik* and salt to taste. Stir through, then add yam and cook, stirring regularly, until both chicken and yam are tender.
- Stir in both chillies and dish out. Garnish and serve as desired.

ASAM CHICKEN
TANGY CHICKEN STEW

INGREDIENTS

Cooking oil	4 Tbsp
Chicken	8 pieces, each about 7.5 x 5 cm (3 x 2 in)
Coconut cream (see pg 31)	500 ml (16 fl oz / 2 cups)
Tamarind (*asam Jawa*) juice (see pg 32)	4 Tbsp
Pineapple	½, peeled, cored and cut into small chunks
Polygonum (*laksa*) leaves (see pg 42)	a handful, chopped + extra for garnishing
Salt	to taste
Sugar	to taste

SPICE PASTE

Shallots	10, peeled
Garlic	4 cloves, peeled
Lemon grass (*serai*)	2 stalks, sliced
Turmeric (*kunyit*)	2-cm (1-in) knob, peeled
Kaffir lime leaves (*daun limau purut*)	4, central stems removed
Dried prawn (shrimp) paste (*belacan*)	2 tsp, dry-roasted (see pg 22)
Chilli paste (*cili boh*) (see pg 85)	5 Tbsp
Ground coriander (*ketumbar serbuk*)	1 Tbsp

METHOD

- Combine all spice paste ingredients in a blender (processor) until smooth.
- Heat oil in a deep pan or pot. Fry spice paste over low heat until fragrant. Add chicken and stir until well-coated with pan ingredients. Cook chicken, stirring regularly, for 10 minutes. Add a little water to prevent sticking, if necessary.
- Add coconut cream and tamarind juice, then add just enough water to cover chicken. Stir through and bring to a simmer. Cook, stirring regularly, for 30 minutes.
- Add pineapple and polygonum leaves. Season to taste with salt and sugar. Continue to simmer until pineapple is slightly softened.
- Dish out and garnish as desired with extra polygonum leaves. Serve warm with plain rice.

AYAM PANGGANG MADURA

GRILLED CHICKEN, MADURA STYLE

Note

This dish is traditionally prepared with palm oil, which is orangy-red in colour and has a strong and distinctive flavour. However, the spotlight on better health in recent years has led many people to shun it, as they have coconut oil, in favour of regular vegetable oils. This is because palm oil has an unusually high fat content, at nearly 80 per cent. Somewhat ironically, palm oil gets its deep, rich colour from carotenes, the same pigment found and sought-after in carrots.

INGREDIENTS

Palm or vegetable oil	4 Tbsp
Chicken	1, about 1.5 kg (3 lb 4½ oz), cleaned and halved lengthways
Coconut milk (see pg 60)	2 litres (64 fl oz / 8 cups)
Screwpine (*pandan*) leaves	3, bruised and tied in a knot
Lemon grass (*serai*)	2 stalks, bruised
Honey	2 Tbsp
Pineapple	½, peeled, cored and cut into cubes
Kerisik (see pg 26)	6 Tbsp
Salt	to taste
Sugar	to taste
Lime (*limau nipis*)	1, squeezed for juice

SPICE PASTE

Red chillies	8, seeded, if desired, and sliced
Bird's eye chillies (*cili padi*)	6, peeled, if desired, and sliced
Candlenuts (*buah keras*)	6
Shallots	10, peeled
Garlic	3 cloves, peeled
Galangal (*lengkuas*)	1-cm (½-in) knob, peeled
Turmeric (*kunyit*)	1-cm (½-in) knob, peeled

WHOLE SPICES

Cinnamon (*kayu manis*)	2-cm (1-in) stick
Cardamoms (*bunga pelaga*)	4 pods or to taste
Cloves (*bunga cengkih*)	4 or to taste

METHOD

- Combine all spice paste ingredients in a blender (processor) until smooth.

- Heat oil in a large pot and fry spice paste over medium-low heat until fragrant. Add chicken halves, increase heat to medium and stir until they are well-coated with pan ingredients. Cook chicken, stirring and turning occasionally, for about 10 minutes.

- Add coconut milk, screwpine leaves, lemon grass, honey, pineapple and whole spices. Bring to a simmer, then reduce heat to low and cook slowly for 40 minutes or until gravy is thickened. Stir frequently.

- Add *kerisik* and cook, stirring, for a further 10 minutes, then season to taste with salt and sugar. Add lime juice and switch off heat.

- Remove chicken from gravy and grill (broil) over hot charcoal for 10 minutes, basting with gravy in the pot and turning from time to time. Alternatively, oven-grill for similar effect.

- Put grilled chicken on a serving plate and spoon gravy over it or onto the side. Garnish and serve as desired.

CHICKEN KUZI

Note

I was fourteen years old when I served this dish for the first time. I was preparing the lauk pengantin *for a Malay wedding and the bride was none other than the sister of my best friend, Razif. The dish turned out to be delicious and has since become a signature dish for me when I am invited to cook at wedding events. It is all right to use ready-packed biryani spices for this recipe, and they are readily available at most supermarkets or Asian shops.*

INGREDIENTS

Chicken	1, about 1.5 kg (3 lb 4½ oz), cleaned and cut into 12 pieces
Garlic	3 cloves, peeled and pounded with 1 tsp salt
Cooking oil	250 ml (8 fl oz / 1 cup)
Shallots	15, peeled and finely sliced
Onions	2, peeled and diced
Almond slivers	20 g (¾ oz / ½ cup)
Raisins	80 g (3 oz / ½ cup)
Chicken liver	1, cut into bite-size pieces
Chicken gizzard	1, cut into bite-size pieces
Salt	to taste
Sugar	to taste

SAUCE

Shallots	5, peeled and pounded into a paste
Garlic	5 cloves, peeled and pounded into a paste
Ground biryani spices	4 Tbsp, mixed with water into a creamy paste
Water	125 ml (4 fl oz / ½ cup)
Evaporated milk	1 can, about 410 g (13½ oz)
Tomato purée	1 can, about 140 g (4½ oz), or 1 bottle tomato sauce (ketchup), about 325 g (11 oz) for a sweeter taste
Lemon grass (*serai*)	2 stalks, bruised
Screwpine (*pandan*) leaves	3, bruised and tied in a knot

GARNISHING

Almond slivers	a handful
Coriander leaves (cilantro)	a handful, chopped

METHOD

- Rub chicken pieces with seasoned garlic and set aside to marinate.

- Line a large tray with several layers of paper towels and heat oil in a wok. Fry shallot slices over low heat until golden brown and crisp. Remove using a slotted spoon with narrow gaps or deep-frying sieve and transfer to tray to drain.

- In the same oil, separately fry onions and almond slivers until just brown; remove to tray. Add raisins and fry briefly, about 5 seconds; remove to tray. Add liver and gizzard and fry until cooked; remove to tray. Lastly, fry marinated chicken pieces to seal in juices and brown lightly, about 5 minutes; remove to tray.

- Prepare sauce. Fry shallot and garlic pastes until fragrant in remaining oil. Add biryani spice paste and fry until fragrant again. Add all remaining ingredients and stir through.

- Reserve some crisp-fried shallots for garnishing, then add all remaining pre-fried ingredients to the sauce. Stir until well-mixed and simmer over low heat for about 30 minutes or until sauce is thickened and chicken tender.

- Season to taste with salt and sugar. Dish out and garnish as desired with reserved crisp-fried shallots, almond slivers and chopped coriander. Serve warm with plain rice or bread.

CHICKEN IN CASHEW SAUCE

INGREDIENTS

Chicken breast or thigh meat	500 g (1 lb 1½ oz), cut into bite-size pieces
Salt	to taste
Ground white pepper	to taste
Ground turmeric (*kunyit serbuk*)	1 tsp
Ground fennel (*jintan manis serbuk*)	1 tsp
Garlic	50 g (2 oz), peeled and minced
Ginger	25 g (1 oz), peeled and minced
Cooking oil	4 Tbsp + enough for shallow- or deep-frying
Butter or margarine	50 g (2 oz)
Onions	100 g (3½ oz), peeled and minced
Curry leaves	10 g (⅓ oz)
Dried chilli	1, rinsed clean, soaked in water to soften and sliced
Thyme	10 g (⅓ oz)
Cashew nuts	100 g (3½ oz), dry-roasted (see pg 35)
Chicken stock (see pg 16)	125 ml (4 fl oz / ½ cup)
Whipping cream	125 ml (4 fl oz / ½ cup)
Green or red capsicum (bell pepper)	30 g (1 oz), seeded, white pith removed and sliced
Tomato	1, sliced

GARNISHING

Coriander leaves (cilantro)	10 g (⅓ oz)
Spring onions (scallions)	10 g (⅓ oz), sliced

METHOD

- Season chicken with salt and pepper, as well as a little of each of the following: turmeric, fennel, garlic and ginger. Leave to marinate for 15 minutes.
- Shallow- or deep-fry marinated chicken in hot oil until cooked, then remove and drain on paper towels.
- Put 4 Tbsp oil and butter or margarine in a pan and heat until solid fat is completely liquid and hot.
- Add onions, curry leaves, dried chilli and thyme, as well as remaining turmeric, fennel, garlic and ginger. Fry until well-mixed and fragrant.
- Add cashew nuts and fry for about 3–4 minutes more, then add stock and simmer for 5 minutes.
- Remove pan from heat and leave contents to cool slightly before transferring to a blender (processor) to purée.
- Pour puréed sauce into a clean saucepan and heat through. Add fried chicken and cream. Stir through and leave to simmer for about 5 minutes.
- Meanwhile, sauté capsicum and tomato slices in an oiled pan until just softened, then add to sauce and stir through.
- Adjust seasoning to taste with salt and pepper before dishing out. Garnish as desired with coriander leaves and spring onions, and serve warm.

MEAT

QUICK COOKING MUSSAMAN BEEF

Note

Mussaman *is a traditional Thai curry that takes hours of simmering to prepare. This dish re-creates the rich flavours of a mussaman curry in its sauce, but because it is more like a stir-fried dish than a slow-cooked curry, it can be brought from the stove to the table in a fraction of the time.*

INGREDIENTS

Potatoes	3, peeled and cut into wedges
Cooking oil for deep-frying	
Lemon grass (*serai*)	2 stalks, bruised
Galangal (*lengkuas*)	1-cm (½-in) knob, peeled and sliced
Beef top round (topside)	400 g (14 oz), sliced
Onion	1, peeled and sliced
Tomatoes	2, cut into wedges
Kaffir lime leaves (*daun limau purut*)	3–4, torn or bruised, or basil leaves
Bird's eye chillies (*cili padi*)	10 or to taste, diagonally halved crossways or leave whole

SPICE PASTE

Red chillies	5, seeded, if desired, and thickly sliced
Shallots	6, peeled
Garlic	3 cloves, peeled

DRY SPICES

Ground coriander (*ketumbar serbuk*)	1 Tbsp
Ground fennel (*jintan manis serbuk*)	1 Tbsp
Ground cinnamon (*kayu manis serbuk*)	½ tsp
Ground star anise (*bunga lawang serbuk*)	½ tsp

SEASONING

Oyster sauce	2 Tbsp
Light soy sauce	1 Tbsp
Fish sauce	3 Tbsp or to taste
Sugar	2 Tbsp or to taste

METHOD

- Combine all spice paste ingredients in a blender (processor) and pulse several times to chop coarsely. Alternatively, coarsely pound using a mortar and pestle. Set aside.

- Heat sufficient oil for deep-frying in a deep pan or wok. Add potato wedges and fry until golden brown. Remove with a slotted spoon and drain on paper towels.

- Remove excess oil from pan, leaving about 2 Tbsp behind. Add spice paste, dry spices, lemon grass and galangal. Fry over medium-low heat until fragrant.

- Add beef and all remaining ingredients, including fried potatoes and seasoning ingredients. Stir-fry until well-mixed and cook for about 3 minutes or until vegetables are just softened. Add a little water, if dry, and adjust to taste with more fish sauce or sugar, if necessary.

- Dish out and serve with plain rice.

THAI MINCED BEEF STIR-FRY WITH BASIL

Note

In Thailand, this stir-fried dish is typically served with rice and an egg, fried sunny-side up, as well as with a selection of fresh herbs and raw vegetables on the side. The Thais generally prefer to use holy basil (bai kra prao) for this dish. Holy basil, unlike regular basil, has rounder leaves with jagged edges. Holy basil is also much more intense in flavour than regular basil and does not become as muted with cooking.

INGREDIENTS

Cooking oil	2 Tbsp
Garlic	4 cloves, peeled and chopped
Bird's eye chillies (*cili padi*)	4, sliced
Minced beef	100 g (3½ oz)
Chicken stock (see pg 16)	3 Tbsp
Basil leaves	2 sprigs

SEASONING

Oyster sauce	1 Tbsp
Dark soy sauce	¼ tsp
Fish sauce	1 Tbsp
Sugar	½ tsp

GARNISHING (OPTIONAL)

Iceberg lettuce leaves

Fresh pineapple pieces

Lime (*limau nipis*) halves

METHOD

- Heat oil in a wok and fry garlic until fragrant, then add chillies and beef. Stir-fry until beef changes colour.

- Add stock and seasoning ingredients. Stir-fry to mix well and adjust seasoning to taste, if necessary.

- Add basil and stir-fry for 30 seconds more, then switch off heat and dish out. Garnish, if using, as desired with iceberg lettuce, pineapple slices and lime halves. Serve warm with rice.

THAI BEEF WITH GREEN PEPPERCORNS

Note

This dish is mildly spicy from the peppercorns and not the chillies because the chillies have been left whole. Slice the chillies, if you prefer a fiery taste. Also, when cooking this dish, be sure to act quickly after you add the basil because it cooks in a flash, and turns black when overcooked. Stir-fry briskly once or twice after adding basil and switch off heat immediately. The basil leaves will cook in the residual heat.

INGREDIENTS

Cooking oil	2 Tbsp
Garlic	2 cloves, peeled and minced
Bird's eye chillies (*cili padi*)	6, left whole
Lean beef	80 g (3 oz), sliced
Chicken stock (see pg 16)	3 Tbsp
Yellow capsicum (bell pepper)	1, seeded, white pith removed and sliced
Kaffir lime leaf (*daun limau purut*)	1, central stem removed and finely sliced
Fresh green peppercorns	5 stems
Basil leaves	10, preferably holy basil (*bai kra prao*) (see pg 135)

SEASONING

Oyster sauce	2 tsp
Light soy sauce	1 tsp
Fish sauce	1 tsp
Sugar	½ tsp

METHOD

- Heat oil in a wok until very hot, then add garlic and chillies. Fry for about 30 seconds or until fragrant.
- Add beef and stir-fry briskly for 1 minute, then add stock, capsicum and seasoning ingredients. Stir-fry to mix well.
- Add lime leaf and peppercorns. Stir-fry for 5 seconds to mix them in, then add basil and stir-fry for 1 second more. Switch off heat.
- Dish out, garnish as desired and serve hot with rice.

INDONESIAN BLACK NUT RENDANG
THICK BEEF STEW WITH INDONESIAN BLACK NUTS

INGREDIENTS

Stewing beef	1.5 kg (3 lb 4½ oz), cleaned and cut into bite-size cubes
Fennel seeds (*jintan manis biji*)	4 tsp, dry-roasted (see pg 35) and finely pounded
Coriander seeds (*ketumbar biji*)	4 tsp
Chilli paste (*cili boh*) (see pg 85)	4 tsp
Coconut milk (see pg 60)	1 litre (32 fl oz / 4 cups), preferably squeezed from 1 grated coconut with sufficient water added
Tamarind (*asam Jawa*) juice (see pg 32)	4 Tbsp or to taste
Palm sugar (*gula Melaka*)	2.5-cm (1-in) piece or to taste, grated
Salt	to taste
Kerisik (see pg 26)	4 tsp

SPICE PASTE

Indonesian black nuts (*buah keluak*)	150 g (5 oz), extracted from hard shells
Red chillies	10, seeded, if desired, and thickly sliced
Shallots	1 kg (2 lb 3 oz), peeled
Garlic	4 cloves, peeled
Ginger	4-cm (2-in) knob, peeled and sliced
Galangal (*lengkuas*)	4-cm (2-in) knob, peeled and sliced
Turmeric (*kunyit*)	2-cm (1-in) knob, peeled and sliced
Lemon grass (*serai*)	4 stalks, sliced
Candlenuts (*buah keras*)	2

METHOD

- Combine all spice paste ingredients in a blender (processor) until smooth.

- Put beef in a large mixing bowl. Add fennel seeds, coriander seeds, chilli paste and spice paste. Mix well and refrigerate, covered, for at least 1 hour to marinate.

- Transfer marinated beef to a pot. Add coconut milk and stir through. Bring to a simmer over medium-low heat and cook, stirring frequently, for 1–1½ hours or until beef is tender. When stirring, be sure to scrape the bottom and sides of the pot to prevent sticking and burning.

- Add tamarind juice, sugar and salt to taste, then stir in *kerisik*. Continue to simmer until gravy is thick and clings to the meat. Dish out and serve with rice.

SERUNDING DAGING
BEEF FLOSS

Note

This classic Malay dish is traditionally served with compressed rice cakes—lontong or ketupat. Today, most supermarkets and Asian stores sell ready-made lontong in the refrigerated section. It is cylindrical in shape, typically wrapped in banana leaf and vacuum-packed. Ketupat, on the other hand, is squarish and wrapped in woven coconut leaves. Apart from shape, the two are virtually the same and can be used interchangeably.

INGREDIENTS

Beef	1 kg (2 lb 3 oz), cut into bite-size cubes
Coconut milk (see pg 60)	1 litre (32 fl oz / 4 cups), preferably squeezed from 2 grated coconuts with sufficient water added
Sugar	2 Tbsp to taste
Salt	to taste

SPICE PASTE

Shallots	20, peeled
Garlic	5 cloves, peeled
Ginger	2.5-cm (1-in) knob, peeled
Lemon grass (*serai*)	5 stalks, sliced
Dried chillies	15, rinsed clean, soaked in water to soften and drained
Coriander seeds (*ketumbar biji*)	2 Tbsp
Fennel seeds (*jintan manis biji*)	1½ tsp

METHOD

• Put beef cubes in a pot of salted water. Bring to the boil over medium heat and simmer until they are tender. Drain beef using a colander and allow to cool.

• Meanwhile, combine all spice paste ingredients in a blender (processor) until smooth. Set aside.

• Shred cooled beef and place in a wok. Add spice paste and coconut milk. Stir through and bring to a boil over medium heat and simmer, stirring constantly, until mixture has no visible liquid.

• Reduce heat to low and stir-fry beef until the shreds break down further to resemble fibres. Add sugar and salt to taste. Switch off heat.

• Serve warm or at room temperature. It is traditionally eaten with compressed rice cakes, called *lontong* or *ketupat* (see note), but makes an especially tasty snack when eaten on its own.

RENDANG PEDAS DAGING

THICK SPICY BEEF STEW

INGREDIENTS

Cooking oil	4 Tbsp
Onions	2, peeled and finely pounded
Beef sirloin	500 g (1 lb 1½ oz), cut into bite-size cubes
Tamarind (*asam Jawa*) juice (see pg 32)	2 Tbsp or to taste
Sugar	to taste
Salt	to taste
Turmeric leaves (*daun kunyit*)	2, washed and sliced

SPICE PASTE

Shallots	8, peeled
Garlic	5 cloves, peeled
Young ginger	2.5-cm (1-in) knob, peeled
Galangal (*lengkuas*)	1-cm (½-in) knob, peeled
Dried chillies	10, rinsed clean, soaked in water to soften and drained
Lemon grass (*serai*)	3 stalks, sliced
Dried prawn (shrimp) paste (*belacan*)	1-cm (½-in) piece, dry-roasted (see pg 22)

METHOD

- Combine all spice paste ingredients in a blender (processor) until smooth.
- Heat oil in a wok or large pan. Fry onions and spice paste over low heat for about 10 minutes, stirring constantly.
- Add beef, tamarind juice, sugar and salt to taste, then add turmeric leaves. Continue to stir constantly until beef is cooked and gravy is thickened.
- Remove from heat, dish out and serve with rice.

CHEF WAN'S SPECIAL MUTTON CURRY

INGREDIENTS

Ghee (clarified butter)	110 g (4 oz / ½ cup)
Curry leaves	4 sprigs
Mutton top round (topside)	1 kg (2 lb 3 oz), sliced
Tomatoes	2, quartered
Whipping cream	250 ml (8 fl oz / 1 cup)
Plain yoghurt	125 ml (4 fl oz / ½ cup)
Sugar	to taste
Salt	to taste
Coriander leaves (cilantro) (optional)	a handful, chopped

SPICE PASTE

Shallots	15, peeled
Onions	2, peeled and cut into chunks
Ginger	3-cm (1½-in) knob, peeled and sliced
Garlic	6 cloves, peeled
Green chillies	6, seeded, if desired, and thickly sliced
Coriander roots	4
Mint leaves	a handful
Black peppercorns	20

WHOLE SPICES

Cloves	6
Cinnamon (*kayu manis*)	2-cm (1-in) stick
Cardamoms (*buah pelaga*)	6 pods
Star anise (*bunga lawang*)	2 whole

DRY SPICES

Garam masala	1 Tbsp
Ground white pepper	1 tsp
Meat curry powder	3 Tbsp

Chilli powder	2 Tbsp
Ground cumin (*jintan putih serbuk*)	1 Tbsp
Ground coriander (*ketumbar serbuk*)	1 Tbsp

METHOD

- Combine all spice paste ingredients in a blender (processor) until smooth.

- Heat ghee in a deep pan or pot. Add curry leaves, whole spices and spice paste. Fry over low heat for about 10 minutes or until fragrant.

- Mix dry spices with a little water into a paste and add to fried spices together with mutton. Cook, still over low heat and stirring constantly, for about 15 minutes or until mutton is well-coated with pan ingredients and flavours from the spices have penetrated the meat.

- Add just enough water to cover ingredients. Simmer, stirring regularly, for about 1 hour or until mutton is tender.

- Add tomatoes, cream and yoghurt. Season to taste with sugar and salt. Stir in coriander leaves (cilantro), if using, then remove from heat. Dish out and serve with rice or bread.

RICE & NOODLES

SEAFOOD JAMBALAYA

Note

Merguez is a type of spicy sausage that is popular in parts of Europe and North Africa. The sausage is made of lamb and mainly seasoned with harissa, a hot chilli paste. Harissa is what gives the merguez its red colour.

INGREDIENTS

Olive oil	125 ml (4 fl oz / ½ cup)
Spicy sausages	2, cut into 2 cm (1 in) pieces, preferably merguez
Green capsicum (bell pepper)	½, seeded, white pith removed and cut into squares
Celery	½ stick, chopped
Onion	1, peeled and chopped
Garlic	3 cloves, peeled and minced
Tomato purée	2 Tbsp
Canned plum (Roma) tomatoes	1 can, about 410 g (13½ oz), crushed
Stock	2.5 litres (4 pints / 10 cups), use fish (see pg 13) or chicken (see pg 16)
Long-grain rice	600 g (1 lb 5 oz / 3 cups), washed and drained
Chopped spring onions (scallions)	125 g (4½ oz)

SEASONING

Thyme	3 sprigs
Oregano	2 sprigs
Basil leaves	a handful
Ground white pepper	2 tsp
Cayenne pepper	3 tsp
Ground black pepper	1½ tsp
Salt	to taste

SEAFOOD

Large prawns (shrimps)	4, deveined and rinsed clean
Green mussels	4, scrubbed clean
Crabs	2, top shells removed, pincers separated, bodies quartered and rinsed clean

METHOD

- Heat oil in a large pan and fry sausages for 10 minutes over medium-high heat, stirring frequently.

- Reduce heat to medium and add capsicum, celery, onion and garlic. Stir for 15 minutes or until browned, scraping up any brown that sticks to the pan; this is essential for flavour.

- Add tomato purée, canned tomatoes and stock. Stir through and bring to the boil, then reduce heat to low and add seasoning ingredients. Allow to simmer for 1 hour.

- Add rice, cover pan and simmer for 15 minutes. Mix in seafood and cook for 5 minutes more or until both seafood and rice are cooked.

- Mix in spring onions just before serving.

KEBULI RICE

Note

Cooking rice in a pot can be tricky because the amount of water needed is not consistent, and heat control is very important. If rice is too moist for your liking at the end of simmering, further reduce heat to very low and allow rice to dry out for 5 minutes before switching off heat. Alternatively, you could transfer the rice, after frying it in oil, to a rice cooker. Add stock, which should rise to about 2 cm (1 in) above the levelled rice, butter and salt, then set to cook.

INGREDIENTS

Chicken	1, about 1.5 kg (3 lb 4½ oz), cleaned and cut into 6–8 pieces
Ground turmeric (*kunyit serbuk*)	to taste
Salt	to taste
Water	3.5 litres (5⅗ pints / 14 cups)
Cooking oil	125 ml (4 fl oz / ½ cup)
Long-grain rice	800 g (1¾ lb / 4 cups), washed and drained
Butter	100 g (3½ oz), cut into small cubes
Crisp-fried shallots (see pg 26)	3 Tbsp or more to taste
Coriander leaves (cilantro)	a handful, chopped

SPICE PASTE

Onion	1, small, peeled and cut into chunks
Shallots	10, peeled
Ginger	2-cm (1-in) knob, peeled and sliced
Lemon grass (*serai*)	4 stalks, sliced
Coriander seeds (*ketumbar biji*)	1 tsp
Black peppercorns	10

METHOD

- Rub chicken pieces all over with turmeric and salt to taste. Set aside, preferably covered and in the refrigerator, for 4–8 hours to marinate.
- Meanwhile, prepare spice paste. Combine all ingredients in a blender (processor) until smooth and set aside.
- Bring water to the boil in a large pot. Add spice paste and chicken pieces. Stir through and simmer for about 15 minutes or until chicken is cooked. Remove chicken and drain well. Strain stock and reserve.
- Heat oil in a heavy deep pan or pot. Brown chicken pieces on both sides over medium heat. Remove and drain on paper towels. Add rice to remaining oil in pan and fry for 3–4 minutes, then add 1.5 litres (48 fl oz / 6 cups) reserved stock, butter and a pinch of salt. Stir through and bring to the boil.
- Reduce heat to low, cover pan and simmer for 12–15 minutes or until all the liquid has been absorbed and rice is nearly cooked. Switch off heat and allow rice to rest, covered, for 10 minutes before serving.
- To serve, scoop a portion of rice onto a serving plate and top with a piece of chicken, then sprinkle crisp-fried shallots and coriander leaves (cilantro) over.

CURRIED RICE
WITH CHICKEN

Note

The chicken in this dish is mainly cooked by the steam that rises from the rice cooking below it. Thus, it is important to cut the chicken into small cubes, about 1 cm (½ in). Larger pieces of chicken will require a longer cooking time, which may cause the rice to dry out too much or burn. Also, do not lift the lid of the pan unnecessarily after switching off the heat because the residual heat forms part of the cooking process for the ingredients on top.

INGREDIENTS

Ghee (clarified butter)	1 Tbsp
Cooking oil	3 Tbsp
Screwpine (*pandan*) leaf	1, washed and knotted
Curry leaves	2 sprigs, stems discarded
Meat curry powder	2 Tbsp
Long-grain rice	600 g (1 lb 5 oz / 3 cups), preferably basmati, washed and drained
Milk	500 ml (16 fl oz / 2 cups)
Chicken stock (see pg 16)	750 ml (24 fl oz / 3 cups)
Salt	to taste
Chicken breasts	2, skinned, boned and cut into small cubes
Mint leaves	3 sprigs
Cashew nuts	5 Tbsp, dry-roasted (see pg 35)
Tomato	1, chopped

SPICE PASTE

Shallots	3, peeled
Garlic	2 cloves, peeled
Ginger	2.5-cm (1-in) knob, peeled
Dried chillies	3, rinsed clean, soaked in water to soften and drained

WHOLE SPICES

Cinnamon (*kayu manis*)	5-cm (2-in) stick
Cardamoms (*buah pelaga*)	5 pods
Star anise (*bunga lawang*)	3 whole or to taste
Cloves (*bunga cengkih*)	5 or to taste

GARNISHING (OPTIONAL)

Carrot	½, peeled, if desired, and julienned
Crisp-fried shallots (see pg 26)	to taste

METHOD

- Combine all spice paste ingredients in a blender (processor) until smooth.

- Heat ghee and oil in a deep pan or pot. Add screwpine and curry leaves, spice paste and whole spices. Fry over medium heat until browned and fragrant, then add curry powder and stir for 5 minutes or until well-mixed.

- Add rice and stir for another 5 minutes until grains are well-coated with pan ingredients. Add milk, stock and salt to taste. Stir through and bring to the boil.

- Reduce heat to low, cover pan and simmer for about 15 minutes or until all the liquid has been absorbed and rice is nearly cooked.

- Distribute chicken, mint leaves, cashew nuts and tomato evenly over rice. Continue to cook over low heat for 5–7 minutes. Switch off heat and allow rice to rest, covered, for about 10 minutes before serving.

- Fluff rice up with a fork before dishing out. Garnish, if using, as desired with julienned carrot and crisp-fried shallots. Serve warm.

NASI ULAM ISTIMEWA
SPECIAL HERBED RICE

Note

For the Malays, ulam *or herbs play a significant role in everyday life, and this was my grandmother's favourite lunch recipe during her confinement period. My version, crystallised after years of revision, uses coconut-flavoured rice that has been dyed yellow by turmeric instead of plain rice.* Budu *is made from fermented anchovies and a pungent condiment. It is sold in bottles at certain supermarkets and provision shops. If unavailable, omit it from the recipe.*

INGREDIENTS

Chubb mackerel (*ikan kembung*)	1, cleaned
Cooking oil for shallow-frying	
Dried prawns (shrimps) (*hae be*)	4 Tbsp, rinsed clean, soaked in water to soften and drained
Lemon grass (*serai*)	1 stalk, finely sliced
Kaffir lime leaves (*daun limau purut*)	2, central stems removed and shredded
Bird's eye chillies (*cili padi*)	3, sliced
Salted egg	1, hard-boiled, shelled and chopped
Shallots	8, peeled and thinly sliced
Kerisik (see pg 26)	70 g (2½ oz)
Kalamansi limes (*limau kesturi*)	4–5, squeezed for juice
Fermented anchovies (*budu*) (optional)	6 Tbsp
Crisp-fried shallots (see pg 26)	30 g (1 oz) or to taste
Salt	to taste

YELLOW COCONUT RICE

Long-grain rice	400 g (13½ oz / 2 cups), preferably basmati, washed and drained
Coconut milk (see pg 60)	750 ml (24 fl oz / 3 cups)
Ginger	1-cm (½-in), peeled and sliced
Galangal (*lengkuas*)	1-cm (½-in), peeled and sliced
Ground turmeric (*kunyit serbuk*)	1 tsp

FINELY SLICED INGREDIENTS

Mint leaves (*daun pudina*)	a handful
Polygonum (*laksa*) leaves (see pg 42)	a handful
Wild cosmos (*ulam raja*)	a handful

Indian pennywort leaves	
(*daun pegaga*)	a handful
Water dropwort leaves	
(*daun selom*)	a handful

METHOD

- Prepare yellow coconut rice. Put rice into a rice cooker and add all remaining ingredients, then set to cook. Fluff up cooked rice with a fork, discarding ginger and galangal slices. Leave rice to cool completely.

- Meanwhile, shallow-fry mackerel in hot oil until cooked and lightly browned on both sides. Remove and drain on paper towels. Dry pre-soaked dried prawns with paper towels and add to hot oil to fry until golden brown and crisp. Remove and drain on paper towels.

- Remove skin of fried mackerel and discard. Separate meat from bones and flake into small pieces. Discard bones and set aside.

- Transfer cooled rice to a large mixing bowl. Add lemon grass, lime leaves, chillies, salted egg, flaked fish and crisp-fried dried prawns. Toss until well-mixed.

- Add raw shallots, *kerisik*, lime juice, fermented anchovies and crisp-fried shallots. Toss until well-mixed again. Repeat with finely sliced ingredients and season to taste with salt. Dish out, then garnish and serve as desired.

BUKHARI RICE
WITH PRAWNS

Note

This dish is one example of Arab influence in Malay cooking. In the Middle East, where slight variations of the dish exist throughout the region, it is usually prepared with lamb or chicken. Bukhari spices are sold ready-ground and -packed in most supermarkets and Asian stores. If preferred, you can transfer the simmered mixture of whole and fresh spices and yoghurt to a rice cooker, then add rice and stock. Set cooker to cook rice and mix in prawns later.

INGREDIENTS

Ghee (clarified butter)	110 g (4 oz / ½ cup)
Garlic	4 cloves, peeled and finely chopped
Prawns (shrimps)	1 kg (2 lb 3 oz), feelers and legs trimmed, deveined and cleaned
Coriander leaves (cilantro)	a handful, finely chopped
Single (light) cream	125 ml (4 fl oz / ½ cup), mixed with juice from 1 lime (*limau nipis*)
Salt	to taste
Sugar	to taste
Saffron threads	a pinch
Screwpine (*pandan*) leaves	2, washed and tied into a knot
Onions	2, peeled and diced
Shallots	10, peeled and finely sliced
Garlic	3 cloves, peeled and finely pounded
Ginger	2-cm (1-in) knob, peeled and finely pounded
Plain yoghurt	250 ml (8 fl oz / 1 cup)
Long-grain rice	800 g (1¾ lb / 4 cups), preferably basmati, washed and drained
Chicken stock (see pg 16)	1.125 litres (36 fl oz / 4½ cups)

DRY SPICES

Ready-packed *bukhari* spices	1 packet
Ground coriander seeds (*ketumbar serbuk*)	1½ Tbsp
Ground black pepper	1 tsp

WHOLE SPICES

Cinnamon	5-cm (2-in) stick
Cloves	5–6 or to taste
Cardamoms	4 pods or to taste
Star anise	2 whole or to taste

GARNISHING

Crisp-fried shallots (see pg 26)	to taste
Coriander leaves (cilantro)	a handful, finely chopped
Red chillies	1–2, seeded, if desired, and sliced

METHOD

- Heat a little ghee in a flat-based pan and fry garlic until lightly browned. Mix dry spices with a little water into a paste and add to pan with prawns and coriander leaves. Fry until fragrant, then stir in a little water and cream. Season to taste with salt and sugar. Remove from heat and set aside.

- Heat remaining ghee in a heavy pot with a snug-fitting lid. Add whole spices, saffron, screwpine leaves, onions, shallots, garlic and ginger. Fry ingredients over medium-low heat until fragrant and lightly browned. Stir in yoghurt and simmer for about 5 minutes.

- Add rice and stir for 2 minutes or until it is well-mixed with spices and yoghurt. Add stock and stir through, then season to taste with salt. Bring to the boil, reduce heat to low and simmer until all the liquid has been absorbed and rice is nearly cooked, about 15 minutes.

- Fluff up rice with a fork and mix in prawns and pan juices. Reduce heat to very low, cover pot and continue cooking for another 5–7 minutes or until rice is cooked. Switch off heat.

- Dish out and garnish as desired with crisp-fried shallots, coriander leaves and red chillies. Serve warm.

HUNAS FRIED RICE

Note

This recipe was created in 2002, when I was filming a cooking show sponsored by Ayam Mas in Sri Lanka. We were up in the Kandy Hills, where tea, cloves and cardamoms are grown in abundance. The weather was cool and as we walked, I saw the Hunas Falls, a beautiful waterfall nestled among rolling hills. The spectacular view inspired me to prepare this dish using ingredients common in Sri Lankan cuisine and name it after the area.

INGREDIENTS

Cooking oil for shallow- or deep-frying	
Potatoes	2, peeled and diced
Chicken breast or thigh meat	500 g (1 lb 1½ oz), sliced into bite-size pieces
Garlic	4 cloves, peeled and finely chopped
Ginger	2-cm (1-in) knob, peeled and finely chopped
Black mustard seeds	1 Tbsp
Curry leaves	2
Meat curry powder	2 Tbsp
Dried prawns (shrimps) (*hae be*)	5 Tbsp, rinsed clean, soaked in water to soften and finely pounded
Cooked rice	950 g (2 lb 2 oz / 4 cups)
Green chillies	4, seeded, if desired, and sliced
Tomatoes	3, seeded and chopped
Cucumber	1, peeled, if desired, cored and chopped
Coriander leaves (cilantro)	1 sprig, chopped
Cashew nuts	70 g (2½ oz / ½ cup), dry-roasted (see pg 35)
Salt	to taste
Ground black pepper	to taste

METHOD

- Heat sufficient oil for shallow-or deep-frying in a deep pan or wok. Add potatoes and fry until golden brown and cooked. Remove and drain on paper towels.

- Remove excess oil from pan, leaving about 2 Tbsp behind. Reheat oil and fry chicken slices until lightly browned. Remove and set aside.

- Heat 4 Tbsp oil in the same pan. Fry garlic, ginger, mustard seeds and curry leaves over medium-low heat until fragrant. Add curry powder and dried prawns. Fry until fragrant again.

- Add rice and stir-fry until well-mixed with pan ingredients. Add fried chicken and potatoes, as well as chillies and tomatoes. Stir-fry until well-mixed again.

- Add cucumber, coriander leaves and cashew nuts. Stir-fry briskly a few times and season to taste with salt and pepper. Switch off heat and dish out, then garnish and serve as desired.

FRIED RICE CAKES

Note

Nasi himpit *is another variety of compressed rice cakes (see pg 141). Unlike log-shaped* lontong *or fist-sized* ketupat, nasi himpit *resembles a thick floor tile, although all three types are similar in taste and texture. Nasi himpit also is cut into smaller pieces to be either served as is or re-cooked as part of a dish. The dark soy sauce used in this recipe is thick like molasses and sweet. If unavailable, use regular dark soy sauce and add a pinch more of sugar.*

INGREDIENTS

Cooking oil	4 Tbsp
Ready-made compressed rice cakes (*nasi himpit*)	600 g (1 lb 5 oz), cut into bite-size pieces
Thick dark soy sauce	½ Tbsp
Garlic	3 cloves, peeled and minced
Chilli paste (*cili boh*) (see pg 85)	½ Tbsp
Eggs	4, lightly beaten
Preserved radish (*chye poh*)	100 g (3½ oz)
Chicken breast or thigh meat	400 g (14 oz), cut into bite-size pieces
Chicken sausages	3, cut into bite-size pieces
Seasoning sauce*	4 Tbsp or to taste
Bean sprouts	400 g (13½ oz), tailed, if desired, and rinsed clean
Chinese chives (*ku cai*)	150 g (5 oz), cut into 2.5-cm (1-in) lengths and rinsed clean

SAUCE

Light soy sauce	50 ml (1¾ fl oz)
Oyster sauce	2 Tbsp
Sugar	2 Tbsp
Salt	1 Tbsp
Water	100 ml (3½ fl oz)
Thick dark soy sauce	1 Tbsp
Chicken stock granules	1 Tbsp

METHOD

- Prepare sauce. Stir all ingredients together until sugar, salt and chicken stock granules are completely dissolved. Adjust to taste, if necessary, and set aside.

- Heat 1 Tbsp oil in a deep pan or wok. Fry rice cakes with thick dark soy sauce until evenly coloured. Remove with a slotted spoon and set aside.

- Reheat pan with remaining oil. Fry garlic and chilli paste over medium heat until fragrant, then add fried rice cakes and stir-fry until evenly mixed.

- Add eggs, preserved radish, chicken, sausages and seasoning sauce to taste. Stir-fry for about 5 minutes or until pan ingredients are well-mixed and chicken is cooked.

- Add bean sprouts and chives. Stir-fry briskly a few times and switch off heat. Dish out and serve immediately.

FRIED TOM YUM RICE VERMICELLI

INGREDIENTS

Cooking oil for shallow-frying	
Chicken breast or thigh meat	300 g (10 oz), sliced into bite-size pieces
Firm bean curd (*tau kwa*)	3 pieces, cut into bite-size pieces
Dried prawns (shrimps) (*hae be*)	75 g (2½ oz / ½ cup), rinsed clean, soaked in water to soften and drained
Oyster sauce	4 Tbsp
Fish sauce	4 Tbsp
Preserved soy bean paste (*taucu*)	2 Tbsp
Sugar	to taste
Rice vermicelli (*bee hoon*)	500 g (1 lb 1½ oz), blanched and drained
Chinese chives (*ku cai*)	10 stalks, cut into 2.5-cm (1-in) lengths
Bean sprouts	200 g (7 oz), tailed, if desired, and rinsed clean
Red chilli	1, seeded, if desired, and sliced

SPICE PASTE

Dried chillies	15, rinsed clean, soaked in water to soften and drained
Lemon grass (*serai*)	1 stalk, sliced
Ginger	1-cm (½-in) knob, peeled and sliced
Galangal (*lengkuas*)	1-cm (½-in) knob, peeled and sliced
Dried prawns (shrimps) (*hae be*)	75 g (2½ oz / ½ cup), rinsed clean, soaked in water to soften and drained
Dried prawn (shrimp) paste (*belacan*)	2 tsp, dry-roasted (see pg 22)
Coriander leaves (cilantro)	5 sprigs
Kaffir lime leaves (*daun limau purut*)	2, central stems discarded
Garlic	3 cloves, peeled
Shallots	8, peeled

METHOD

- Combine all spice paste ingredients in a blender (processor) until smooth. Set aside.

- Heat 1 Tbsp oil in a deep pan or wok. Fry chicken slices until lightly browned. Remove and set aside.

- Add sufficient oil to pan for shallow-frying and reheat. Fry bean curd pieces until golden brown, then remove and drain on paper towels.

- Dry pre-soaked dried prawns with paper towels and add to hot oil to fry until golden brown and crisp. Remove and drain on paper towels.

- Assess oil left in the pan and either add or remove oil to have about 4 Tbsp inside. Reheat oil and fry spice paste until fragrant. Add oyster and fish sauces, soy bean paste and sugar to taste. Stir until well-blended.

- Add vermicelli and a little water. Stir-fry until vermicelli is well-mixed with pan ingredients. While stir-frying, it may be necessary to keep adding small amounts of water to prevent the vermicelli from drying out; at no point should the vermicelli be hard and brittle.

- Add fried bean curd and chicken, chives and bean sprouts. Stir-fry until well-mixed, then switch off heat. Dish out, sprinkle with crisp-fried dried prawns and chilli to garnish and serve.

MUM'S MEE BANDUNG

Note

This is my family's second favourite noodle dish, after my grandmother's mee rebus, which was featured in Simply Sedap!. My mother often prepared mee bandung for the family to break fast during Ramadan, the Islamic fasting month. It was also one of the more popular dishes in the cafeteria that she ran in an airbase for the Royal Malaysian Air Force in Alor Star, Kedah.

INGREDIENTS

Cooking oil for shallow- or deep-frying	
Firm bean curd (*tau kwa*)	1 piece
Eggs	2
Shallots	3, peeled and sliced
Garlic	4 cloves, peeled and minced
Ginger	2-cm (1-in) knob, peeled and minced
Chilli paste (*cili boh*) (see pg 85)	2 Tbsp
Chicken stock (see pg 16)	500 ml (16 fl oz / 2 cups)
Prawns (shrimps)	200 g (7 oz), shelled and deveined
Squid tubes	200 g (7 oz), cut as desired
Tomato sauce (ketchup)	125 ml (4 fl oz / ½ cup)
Thai roasted chilli paste (*nam prik phao*)	2 Tbsp
Cabbage	100 g (3½ oz), shredded
Chinese flowering cabbage (*chye sim*)	3 stalks, cut into 3-cm (1½-in) lengths
Fishballs	6
Bean sprouts	a handful, tailed, if desired
Yellow (Hokkien) noodles	200 g (7 oz), blanched and drained
Salt	to taste

GARNISHING

Crisp-fried shallots (see pg 26)	to taste
Red chillies	2–3, seeded, if desired, and sliced
Green chillies	2, seeded, if desired, and sliced
Spring onions (scallions)	2–3, diagonally sliced
Coriander leaves (cilantro)	a handful, chopped

164 SIMPLY SEDAP 2

METHOD

- Heat sufficient oil for shallow- or deep-frying in a deep pan or wok. Add bean curd pieces and fry until golden brown. Remove and drain on paper towels. Cut cooled bean curd into small cubes.

- Remove excess oil from pan, leaving about 4 Tbsp behind. Reheat oil and fry each egg into a sunny-side up. Dish out and set aside.

- Assess oil left in the pan and add sufficient oil to have about 4 Tbsp inside. Reheat oil and fry shallots, garlic and ginger until fragrant. Add chilli paste and fry for 1 minute.

- Add stock, seafood, tomato sauce and Thai roasted chilli paste. Stir through, then add cabbage, Chinese flowering cabbage, fishballs, bean sprouts, noodles and fried bean curd. Stir until pan ingredients are well-mixed and season to taste with salt.

- When seafood is cooked, switch off heat. Transfer to individual serving bowls and top with fried eggs. Garnish as desired with crisp-fried shallots, red and green chillies, spring onions and coriander leaves. Serve immediately.

MEE REBUS

INGREDIENTS

Cooking oil	125 ml (4 fl oz / ½ cup)
Meat curry powder	60 g (2 oz / ½ cup)
Chicken breast or thigh meat	450 g (1 lb), cut into bite-size pieces
Preserved soy bean paste (*taucu*)	250 g (8 oz / 1 cup), mashed, if desired
Water	2 litres (64 fl oz / 8 cups)
Sweet potatoes	3, large, boiled in water until cooked, then peeled and mashed
Tomatoes	3, cut into wedges
Ground peanuts (groundnuts)	2 Tbsp or to taste
Salt	to taste
Sugar	to taste
Corn flour (cornstarch)	3 Tbsp, mixed with a 5 Tbsp water
Potatoes (optional)	2, peeled, diced and fried
Yellow (Hokkien) noodles	1 kg (2 lb 3 oz), blanched and drained
Bean sprouts	150 g (5 oz), tailed, if desired and blanched

SPICE PASTE

Shallots	15, peeled
Garlic	4 cloves, peeled
Ginger	4-cm (2-in) knob, peeled

GARNISHING

Hard-boiled eggs	2, shelled and sliced
Firm bean curd (*tau kwa*)	2 pieces, fried and cut into small cubes
Chinese celery or spring onions (scallions)	2 sprigs, chopped
Green chillies	2, seeded, if desired, and sliced
Kalamansi limes (*limau kesturi*)	4 or more to taste, halved
Crisp-fried shallots (see pg 26)	to taste

METHOD

- Combine all spice paste ingredients in a blender (processor) until smooth.

- Heat oil in a pot. Add spice paste and curry powder and fry until fragrant. Add chicken, soy bean paste, water and sweet potatoes. Stir through and bring to the boil.

- Add tomatoes and peanuts, then season to taste with salt and sugar. Stir in corn flour solution and simmer for 5 minutes, stirring constantly, until gravy is thick. Add potatoes, if using, and simmer until they are tender.

- To serve, place some yellow noodles and bean sprouts in each serving bowl, then ladle hot gravy over. Top with desired amounts of each garnishing ingredient.

CURRY NOODLES

INGREDIENTS

Cooking oil for shallow- or deep-frying	
Firm bean curd (*tau kwa*)	2 pieces
Meat curry powder	40 g (1⅓ oz), mixed into a paste with a little of water
Curry leaves	3 sprigs
Chicken breast or thigh meat	250 g (8½ oz), cut into bite-size pieces
Shelled prawns (shrimps)	150 g (5 oz), with tails intact
Ready-made chicken meatballs	200 g (7 oz), halved
Dried sour fruit (*asam gelugur*)	2–3 pieces or more to taste
Coconut milk (see pg 60)	500 ml (16 fl oz / 2 cups)
Water	650 ml
Salt	½ tsp or taste
Tomatoes	2, cut into small wedges
Yellow (Hokkien) noodles	350 g (11½ oz), blanched and drained
Bean sprouts	200 g (7 oz), tailed, if desired, and blanched
Chinese flowering cabbage (*chye sim*)	600 g (1 lb 5 oz), blanched and cut into bite-size pieces
Coriander leaves (cilantro)	3 sprigs, coarsely chopped

WHOLE SPICES

Cinnamon (*kayu manis*)	3-cm (1½-in) stick
Cloves (*bunga cengkih*)	3
Star anise (*bunga lawang*)	1
Cardamoms (*buah pelaga*)	3

SPICE PASTE

Shallots	3, peeled
Garlic	2 cloves, peeled
Ginger	2-cm (1-in) knob, peeled and sliced

METHOD

- Combine all spice paste ingredients in a blender (processor) until smooth. Set aside.

- Heat sufficient oil for shallow- or deep-frying in a deep pan or wok. Add bean curd pieces and fry until golden brown. Remove and drain on paper towels. Cut cooled bean curd into small cubes.

- Remove excess oil from the pan, leaving about 2 Tbsp behind. Reheat oil and fry spice paste and whole spices over low heat until lightly browned. Add curry paste and curry leaves. Stir until fragrant.

- Add chicken pieces and stir until they are well-coated with pan ingredients. Sprinkle in some water, cover and cook over medium heat for about 5 minutes.

- Add prawns, chicken meatballs, dried sour fruit, coconut milk and remaining water. Stir through and simmer for 5 minutes, then season to taste with salt. Cook for 3–4 minutes more before adding tomatoes. Stir through and switch off heat.

- To serve, put some noodles, bean sprouts, Chinese flowering cabbage and fried bean curd into individual serving bowls, then ladle hot gravy over and sprinkle with coriander to garnish. Serve immediately.

FETTUCCINE PESTO PRIMAVERA

Note

I lived in the United States for four years (1986–1990) and during this time, I explored the country's wine regions, including Sonoma and Napa Valley, over weekends in the warmer months. My friends and I would drive to the region we had planned to visit and enjoy a picnic there. This particular recipe is my favourite picnic dish. Served warm or cold, it takes your breath away.

INGREDIENTS

Extra virgin olive oil	4 Tbsp
Garlic	2 cloves, peeled and sliced
Red capsicum (bell pepper)	½, seeded, white pith removed and sliced
Courgette (zucchini)	¼, cut into bite-size pieces
Celery	¼ stalk, chopped
Bird's eye chilli (*cili padi*) (optional)	1, sliced
Ready-made pesto sauce	2 Tbsp
Fettuccine	200 g (7 oz), cooked until al dente
Chicken stock (see pg 16)	4 Tbsp
Salt	½ tsp or to taste
Freshly cracked black pepper	to taste
Grated Parmesan cheese	to taste
Basil leaves	1 small sprig

METHOD

- Heat olive oil in a pan. Add garlic, capsicum, courgette, celery and chilli, if using. Fry for 1 minute, then mix in pesto sauce.
- Add cooked fettuccine and toss until well-mixed before adding stock. Toss a few more times and season to taste with salt and pepper.
- Dish out, sprinkle Parmesan cheese over and garnish as desired with basil leaves. Serve.

SPAGHETTI WITH CHICKEN AND SUN-DRIED TOMATOES

INGREDIENTS

Red capsicum (bell pepper)	½, seeded and white pith removed
Butter	2 Tbsp
Extra virgin olive oil	3 Tbsp
Onion	½, peeled and chopped
Garlic	2 cloves, peeled and chopped
Bird's eye chilli (*cili padi*)	1, chopped
Chicken breast	1, skinned, boned and cut into bite-size pieces
Tomatoes	2, seeded and thinly sliced
Sun-dried tomatoes	6, sliced
Salt	to taste
Freshly cracked black pepper	to taste
Spaghetti	300 g (10 oz), cooked until al dente
Chicken stock (see pg 16)	125 ml (4 fl oz / ½ cup)
Single (light) cream	125 ml (4 fl oz / ½ cup)
Grated Parmesan cheese	2 Tbsp or more to taste

HERBS

Rosemary leaves	1 sprig
Thyme leaves	2 sprigs
Basil leaves	10, thinly sliced

METHOD

- Roast capsicum pieces: place them on a baking tray and roast in a preheated oven at 200°C (400°F) until their skins are charred. Transfer them to a clean plastic bag, seal and leave for 5 minutes. Take them out and rub off the charred skins, then slice into strips and set aside.
- Heat butter and olive oil in a pan. Fry onion, garlic and chilli for 30 seconds or until onion is translucent.
- Add chicken and fry until it changes colour, then add capsicum, both types of tomatoes and herbs. Stir until well-mixed, then season to taste with salt and pepper.
- Add spaghetti, a third at a time, and toss to mix well after each addition. Add stock, a little at a time, while tossing spaghetti.
- When all the stock has been added and spaghetti is well-mixed with pan ingredients, pour cream over and stir through. Dish out, sprinkle cheese over and serve.

BAKED MACARONI

INGREDIENTS

Red capsicum (bell pepper)	1, large, about 200 g (7 oz), quartered, seeded and white pith removed
Chicken breast or thigh meat	300 g (10 oz), cut into bite-size pieces
Ready-made pesto sauce	125 ml (4 fl oz / ½ cup)
Courgettes (zucchini)	2 quartered lengthways and sliced
Chopped basil leaves	2 Tbsp
Grated Parmesan cheese	100 g (3½ oz / 1 cup)
Potatoes	3, peeled and diced
Carrot	1, peeled, if desired, and diced
Macaroni	250 g (9 oz), cooked until al dente
Toasted pine nuts	30 g (1 oz / ¼ cup)
Chicken sausages	8, cut into 0.5-cm (¼-in) thick slices
Double (heavy) cream	300 ml (10 fl oz / 1¼ cups)
Grated mozzarella cheese	125 g (4½ oz / 1 cup)
Onion	1, peeled and sliced
Chopped parsley	3 Tbsp

METHOD

- Oven-roast capsicum pieces (see pg 173) and slice flesh into thin strips. Set aside.
- Into a large bowl, put chicken, pesto, courgettes, basil, Parmesan cheese, potatoes, carrot, capsicum and macaroni. Add half the pine nuts and sausages, then toss until well-mixed.
- Transfer above mixture to a greased casserole dish and spread out evenly with the back of a spoon or spatula. Pour cream all over.
- Into another bowl, put grated mozzarella cheese, onion and parsley, as well as remaining pine nuts and sausages. Mix well, then spoon mixture over macaroni and spread out evenly.
- Put casserole in a preheated oven at 180°C (350°F) and bake for 25 minutes or until most of the cheese is melted and parts of the surface are browned.
- Remove casserole from oven and divide among individual serving plates to serve or serve directly from the casserole.

DESSERTS

CEK MEK MOLEK

SWEET POTATO PUFFS

INGREDIENTS

Sweet potatoes	300 g (10 oz), boiled in water until cooked and peeled
Plain (all-purpose) flour	50 g (1½ oz), sifted
Salt	a pinch
Sugar	50 g (1½ oz)
Cooking oil for deep-frying	
Icing (confectioners') sugar (optional)	

METHOD

- Boil sweet potatoes until cooked, then drain and allow to cool. Peel and finely mash sweet potatoes, removing all fibres to discard.

- Sift flour and salt over mashed sweet potatoes. Mix well and knead lightly into a dough. Add a little water, if dry.

- Pinch a ball of dough roughly 5 cm (2 in) in diameter and make a depression at the centre. Fill with ½ tsp sugar, then gather edges and pinch to seal. Shape to look like a rugby ball, with pointed ends. Repeat until ingredients are used up.

- Deep-fry sweet potato puffs, in small batches, until golden brown. Remove with a slotted spoon and drain on paper towels.

- Dust with icing sugar, if using, and serve warm.

STEAMED JACKFRUIT CUSTARD

Note

To obtain screwpine juice, cut cleaned leaves into shorter lengths and pound with a little water added, then squeeze using a piece of muslin cloth. Alternatively, blend (process) leaves with some water and pass through a fine strainer for similar results.

INGREDIENTS

Grated skinned coconut	300 g (10 oz), about 1 coconut
Screwpine (*pandan*) juice (see note)	extracted from 3–4 leaves
Eggs	6
Sugar	180 g (6 oz / ¾ cup)
Jackfruit pulp	6 pieces, seeded and thinly sliced

METHOD

- Place grated coconut in a large bowl. Add screwpine juice and eggs and mix well.
- Squeeze coconut mixture using a piece of muslin cloth to extract as much liquid as possible. Stir sugar into coconut liquid.
- Line a steaming bowl or individual serving cups with jackfruit, then pour coconut liquid over.
- Steam for 10–15 minutes or until cooked; individual serving cups take less time. Serve warm or chilled.

CHILLED COCONUT CUSTARD

INGREDIENTS

Young coconut	1, husk removed but left whole
Egg	1
Coconut cream (see pg 31)	125 ml (4 fl oz / ½ cup)
Palm sugar (*gula Melaka*)	1½ Tbsp, or granulated sugar
Screwpine (*pandan*) leaf	1
Salt	¼ tsp
Grated skinned coconut (optional)	

METHOD

- Cut off top of coconut and pour out translucent juice inside. Steam coconut bowl for 5 minutes and remove. Keep steamer hot.
- Combine all remaining ingredients in a bowl and stir until well-mixed, then strain mixture into coconut bowl.
- Steam filled coconut bowl for 15–20 minutes or until custard is cooked. To test, insert a skewer into the centre of the custard; it should come out clean.
- Remove cooked custard from steamer and allow to cool completely, then refrigerate until chilled. Sprinkle with grated coconut, if using, just before serving.

PUMPKIN PANCAKES

INGREDIENTS

Pumpkin	800 g (1¾ lb), seeded and stringy fibres removed
Oat bran	130 g (4½ oz)
Plain (all-purpose) flour	140 g (5 oz)
Ground cinnamon (*kayu manis serbuk*)	¼ tsp
Bicarbonate of soda (baking soda)	1 Tbsp
Castor (superfine) sugar	15 g (½ oz)
Low-fat yoghurt	225 g (7½ oz)
Vanilla essence (extract)	1 tsp
Cooking oil	2 Tbsp
Egg whites	135 g (4½ oz), beaten to medium-peak stage (see pg 45)

GARNISHING (OPTIONAL)

Assorted fresh fruit

Mint leaves

Icing (confectioners') sugar

METHOD

- Wrap pumpkin in aluminium foil and bake in a preheated oven at 190°C (370°F) for about 45–50 minutes. Remove baked pumpkin and allow to cool completely.
- Peel baked pumpkin and finely mash, removing all stringy fibres to discard. You should get about 140 g (5 oz) of mash.
- Put oat bran, flour, cinnamon, bicarbonate of soda and sugar in a bowl. Mix well, then add yoghurt, mashed pumpkin, vanilla essence and half the oil. Mix well again before folding in egg whites.
- Grease a griddle or non-stick pan using remaining oil and heat. Spoon ladlefuls (about 4 Tbsp) of batter onto pan and cook until bubbles rise to the surface. Turn pancakes over and cook until golden brown, then remove. Repeat until ingredients are used up.
- Garnish, if using, as desired with fresh fruit, mint leaves and icing sugar. Serve.

GLOSSARY

01 CANDLENUTS

Known to Malay-speakers as *buah keras*, candlenuts are hard, yellow, waxy and largely tasteless. They are generally the size of a shelled walnut and are typically pounded and added to curries to thicken them. If unavailable, use macadamia, brazil or cashew nuts instead. Substitute 1 macadamia nut for 1 candlenut; 1 brazil nut for 2–3 candlenuts; and 2 cashew nuts for 1 candlenut.

02 CARDAMOMS

Extremely strong-tasting, cardamoms are sold in their pods (pictured) or as seeds. The dark seeds, found inside the creamy white pods, are usually added directly to the dish. If using the pods whole, lightly smash them with a knife or press them between your fingertips to release their flavour before adding to the dish. Note that ready-packed cardamom seeds are less flavourful than those still in the pods.

03 CHILLIES

Chillies, both red and green, are used extensively in many Asian cuisines. Generally, the larger the chilli, the milder it is. Of the larger chillies, the red ones taste somewhat sweeter than the green ones. Bird's eye chillies, or *cili padi* (pictured), are rarely longer than 5 cm (2 in) and are especially fiery. Both red and green bird's eye chillies pack a punch.

04 CLOVES

Cloves have a robust flavour and aroma, so much so that only a few are needed each time. Shaped like small nails, cloves are actually dried flower buds and their unique shape allows them to be poked into chunks of meat or pastries to flavour them. Avoid biting into them as they will overpower whatever is being consumed. Cloves are sold whole or ready-ground.

05 COCONUT

The grated flesh of the coconut is flavourful and a little oily. Squeeze it using a piece of muslin cloth with no water added for coconut cream, then add some water and squeeze again for coconut milk. With the wide range of instant coconut cream and milk products available today, however, few people still squeeze their own. Instead, grated coconut is more often used to make what Malay-speakers call *kerisik*—grated coconut that has been dry-roasted over low heat until it is dark brown and deeply aromatic. *Kerisik* is typically used as a flavouring agent in liquid-based dishes or as a flavourful garnishing ingredient, much like crisp-fried shallots.

06 CORIANDER SEEDS

These tiny balls form the backbone of most Indian curries. Although they are called seeds, they are really the dried fruit of the coriander plant (*Coriandrum sativum*). The leaves of the plant also make a flavourful herb, also known as cilantro or Chinese parsley. The Thais are well known for using the root of the plant in their spice pastes as well. Coriander seeds are also sold ground.

07 CUMIN SEEDS

Like coriander, these small, rice-like grains are called seeds even though they are actually the dried fruit of a plant (*Cuminum cyminum*) that belongs to the parsley family. Cumin, which Malay-speakers know it as *jintan putih*, is a key ingredient in ready-made curry powders and is very pungent. Whether whole or ground, use it sparingly.

08 CURRY LEAVES

True to their name, curry leaves give off the distinctive aroma of curry and impart an inimitable peppery flavour to dishes. The plant from which these fragrant leaves grow (*Murraya koenigii*) is native to South Asia.

09 DRIED PRAWN PASTE

Known to Malay-speakers as *belacan*, dried prawn (shrimp) paste is typically sold in the form of rectangular blocks. Be warned that its pungent fishy smell intensifies with dry-roasting, which is often necessary before use. When it has been mixed with some pounded chillies and lime juice, however, the transformation is remarkable. The dried prawn paste becomes an enticing flavouring agent and the mixture makes a great side dip, known as *sambal belacan* in Malaysia and Singapore. The paste is often also added in small quantities to stir-fried dishes and thick, curried stews.

10 DRIED SOUR FRUIT

This ingredient has no common English name, and "dried sour fruit" is a direct translation of *asam gelugur*, its Malay name. When looking for them in the supermarket or shops, be mindful that many suppliers are known to mislabel them as "tamarind pieces" or "tamarind skins" even though the plant from which this fruit is derived is completely unrelated to the tamarind family. These dried slices are added only to liquid-based dishes and, like tamarind, impart sourness to the dish. The longer they have been cooked in the dish, the more sour the dish becomes, so remove them according to taste.

11 FENNEL SEEDS

Also known as sweet cumin or *jintan manis* to Malay-speakers, fennel seeds are pungent and only small quantities are required to impart a sweet fragrance and flavour that is strongly reminiscent of aniseed or licorice to the dish.

12 KAFFIR LIME LEAVES

Kaffir lime leaves, or *daun limau purut* to Malay-speakers, are sometimes known as double lime leaves because of the way they grow on branches. Typically added to liquid-based dishes, such as curries, stews or soups, the leaves are tough and fibrous and can be unpleasant to eat. This is why they are usually used whole but bruised or torn to release their fragrance. Alternatively, they can be finely shredded after removing the central stems.

13 LIMES

Several varieties of limes are sold throughout Southeast Asia. Among them are the common lime (pictured), which Malay-speakers know as *limau nipis*, and a smaller, far more fragrant variety known as kalamansi limes, which Malay-speakers call *limau kesturi*. Another type, the kaffir or Thai lime, has thick and knobbly skin. It does not yield much juice when squeezed but its zest, much like its leaves, impart a subtle but inimitable flavour when added to a dish.

14 PRESERVED SHRIMPS

Better known by its Malay name of *cencaluk*, these preserved shrimps make a feisty and flavourful dip when mixed with some lime juice and sliced chillies. The pinkish condiment, when poured straight out of the bottle, gives off a smell that is disagreeable to most people. Like dried prawn paste (*belacan*), it needs to be combined with other ingredients to bring out its best.

15 PRESERVED SOY BEAN PASTE

Better known as *tau cheo* to Hokkien-speakers or *taucu* to Malay-speakers, preserved soy bean paste was first used as a flavouring agent by early Chinese cooks. Over time, cooks in Southeast Asia, including Singapore, Malaysia and Thailand, discovered the versatility of these salty beans and began to adopt them into their dishes. These beans are sometimes used whole but mostly mashed before they are added to a dish. They are also typically countered with a pinch of sugar for a better balance of flavours.

16 SAFFRON THREADS

Saffron threads (*Crocus sativus*) have the reputation for being the most expensive spice in the world, and it is not difficult to see why. They are the dried stigmas of saffron flowers, and each flower only has a few. Saffron threads, however, are so deeply aromatic that adding just a pinch suffices in making a dish, usually a soup or stew, rich and enticing. They tend also to impart hues of orange and yellow to the dish.

17 TAMARIND PULP

This dark brown, sticky pulp is gathered from pods of the tamarind plant, and within the pulp are many hard seeds. Tamarind pulp is typically used to make tamarind juice, which imparts a sourish flavour to dishes. Tamarind juice is made by mixing a portion of the pulp with water and then straining it. The pulp is rarely used as it is, except when it is part of a marinade.

18 TORCH GINGER BUD

What would otherwise have become a pretty pink flower, the torch ginger bud has a distinct lemony fragrance that does wonders in lifting or adding zest to dishes that may be cloyingly rich after a few mouthfuls. The bud is quite fibrous, however, and is often either used whole and bruised or finely sliced.

19 TURMERIC

Also known as yellow ginger, turmeric is used both for its flavour and its ability to colour a dish bright yellow. It tastes somewhat like a warmer, spicier version of ginger. Some people have even described it as bitter. Handle the orangy yellow flesh of turmeric with care because its juice is notorious for leaving stubborn stains, whether on your fingers, clothes, chopping board or counter top.

20 YAM (TARO)

This fleshy, starchy tuber has pale grey flesh with purple streaks underneath its thin but fibrous brown peel. Its flesh, when cooked, and has a lovely nutty flavour and a texture similar to cooked potatoes. In much of Asia, yams are boiled, mashed and fried in a variety of dishes, much like potatoes in Western cooking. In the U.S., "yam" sometimes refers to orange-fleshed sweet potatoes. Consider candied yams for a case in point.

WEIGHTS AND MEASURES

Quantities for this book are given in Metric, Imperial and American (spoon and cup) measures. Standard spoon and cup measurements used are: 1 tsp = 5 ml, 1 Tbsp = 15 ml, 1 cup = 250 ml. All measures are level unless otherwise stated.

LIQUID AND VOLUME MEASURES

Metric	Imperial	American
5 ml	⅙ fl oz	1 teaspoon
10 ml	⅓ fl oz	1 dessertspoon
15 ml	½ fl oz	1 tablespoon
60 ml	2 fl oz	¼ cup (4 tablespoons)
85 ml	2½ fl oz	⅓ cup
90 ml	3 fl oz	⅜ cup (6 tablespoons)
125 ml	4 fl oz	½ cup
180 ml	6 fl oz	¾ cup
250 ml	8 fl oz	1 cup
300 ml	10 fl oz (½ pint)	1¼ cups
375 ml	12 fl oz	1½ cups
435 ml	14 fl oz	1¾ cups
500 ml	16 fl oz	2 cups
625 ml	20 fl oz (1 pint)	2½ cups
750 ml	24 fl oz (1⅕ pints)	3 cups
1 litre	32 fl oz (1⅗ pints)	4 cups
1.25 litres	40 fl oz (2 pints)	5 cups
1.5 litres	48 fl oz (2⅖ pints)	6 cups
2.5 litres	80 fl oz (4 pints)	10 cups

DRY MEASURES

Metric	Imperial
30 grams	1 ounce
45 grams	1½ ounces
55 grams	2 ounces
70 grams	2½ ounces
85 grams	3 ounces
100 grams	3½ ounces
110 grams	4 ounces
125 grams	4½ ounces
140 grams	5 ounces
280 grams	10 ounces
450 grams	16 ounces (1 pound)
500 grams	1 pound, 1½ ounces
700 grams	1½ pounds
800 grams	1¾ pounds
1 kilogram	2 pounds, 3 ounces
1.5 kilograms	3 pounds, 4½ ounces
2 kilograms	4 pounds, 6 ounces

OVEN TEMPERATURE

	°C	°F	Gas Regulo
Very slow	120	250	1
Slow	150	300	2
Moderately slow	160	325	3
Moderate	180	350	4
Moderately hot	190/200	375/400	5/6
Hot	210/220	410/425	6/7
Very hot	230	450	8
Super hot	250/290	475/550	9/10

LENGTH

Metric	Imperial
0.5 cm	¼ inch
1 cm	½ inch
1.5 cm	¾ inch
2.5 cm	1 inch

ABBREVIATION

tsp	teaspoon
Tbsp	tablespoon
g	gram
kg	kilogram
ml	millilitre